DANGEROUS WATERS

DANGEROUS WATERS

ONE MAN'S
SEARCH FOR ADVENTURE

DAVID PHILPOTT

McCLELLAND AND STEWART

McClelland and Stewart Limited
The Canadian Publishers
25 Hollinger Road, Toronto M4B 3G2

Canadian Cataloguing in Publication Data

Philpott, David.
  Dangerous waters

ISBN 0-7710-6998-7

1. Sailing – Atlantic Ocean.   2. Sailing – Caribbean sea.   3. Rescues – Atlantic Ocean. 4. Adventure and adventurers – Canada. 5. Philpott, David.   I. Title.

G530.P48 1985   910'.09163   C85-099545-0

Printed and bound in Canada by Gagné Ltd.

For Stephen and Wendy

ACKNOWLEDGEMENTS

This book would have remained a loose collection of mini-cassettes and memories if it had not been for:

Joan Hammell, who not only ran my company, cared for me, and suffered my eccentricities, but transcribed over a thousand pages of meandering notes and thoughts into a readable journal.

Beverly Slopen, my agent, confidante, and advocate who guided me through the publishing labyrinth during the past five years.

David Scott, who took my ample diary and structured it, showing me how a professional writer would go about it.

Jinny Harris, my dear friend, who typed at least four final drafts during the past three years and helped me transform a cluster of random essays into a book.

Jack McClelland, who knew the story was good and that I could write it.

Charis Wahl, my editor, who honed and polished my manuscript into that which you are about to read.

The sea voyage required a great deal of planning and co-operation. Bill Wilson of Meridian Marine in Toronto supplied most of my open-sea charts. Gabriel's, in Toronto and Halifax, supplied my charts for the Great Lakes to the East Coast. Also, I am indebted to Mr. Kirsten of the South African Consulate, for putting me in touch with Captain Andrias Gevij of Kerr Steamships (Canada) Limited. He radioed one of his vessels headed down the St. Lawrence and retrieved two excellent charts of Capetown and its approaches.

My father, who considered the King's English, an inquiring mind, and unwavering self-confidence, together with a self-deprecating sense of humour, to be the ultimate menu of life.

Joanne and many, many more.

CHAPTER ONE

*I*HAD COME TO ENJOY THE TIME OF DAY, JUST BEFORE SUNSET, WHEN I WOULD TAKE OFF TO PREPARE my evening meal. On that day, September 7, 1980, I was forty-seven days out of Antigua en route to the Cape of Good Hope, fifty-three years old, in good health and spirits, scudding before a storm in the middle of the South Atlantic. I was directing my limited culinary talents to combining Uncle Ben's rice boiled in V-8 juice with canned Danish sausages. All to be washed down with powdered skimmed milk prepared the day before, and topped off with preserved pears and raisins. It seemed years ago that I was one of the "earth people" who would consider such a supper unfit for a charity soup kitchen. Here in the solitude of wind and water, however, even the anticipation of such a meal was a joy.

Serenity IV rocketed along, seeming to relish the challenge of the giant waves. I'd been on the same course, with the wind on the port quarter, for six days; just a couple of hours earlier I had changed to a starboard tack. With the wind rising and the sun setting, I'd adjusted my self-steering gear and checked the sail before going below to eat.

Suddenly she broached.

It was as though the little thirty-foot catboat had been tripped. As she slid down the face of yet another thirty-foot wave, her stern slewed off to the starboard and she jibed.

For days I had been sailing with the wind almost dead astern, in force five to six winds; and there had always been at least the possibility of an accidental jibe. It can take only an instant. The wind moves in front of the sail and whips it from one side to the other at an incredible speed, quite often carrying away mast and rigging with it. But *Serenity IV* had experienced more than a few accidental jibes in the seven thousand

7

miles and I was reasonably confident that she had come through this one unscathed.

I latched on my safety harness and scrambled up on deck. To my relief the sail and rigging were still intact, but the self-steering gear was seriously damaged. Without this device I would be forced to stay at the helm whenever the boat was under sail, heaving-to when I would have to perform other duties, to eat or to sleep. I had broken many of the plywood vanes before, and I still had twelve reserve blades in the engine room below. But this time the metal casting had also sheared. I felt certain that I could effect the necessary repairs with spare parts, epoxy, and fibreglass, but with the gale building and darkness about one hour away it was more prudent to sit out the storm than attempt to sail through the night at the helm.

I would lie-a-lull: drop sail, make everything fast, and go below, allowing the boat to ride out the storm. The motion below is not particularly comfortable, but it is preferable to exposing a small vessel to the possibility of a knockdown or damage to the sail and rigging.

A few days out of Antigua I realized that my sails were defective: the brass runners that hold the sail to the mast track had been ripping out of the sail with frightening regularity. The sail was now precariously attached to the mast at the bottom and the top only. I had winched the halyard until it was as taut as a piano string to keep the sail from bellying away from the mast. I was about to take a calculated risk. I would round the boat up into the wind to take pressure off the sail. When I loosened the halyard, the canvas should drop cleanly into the lazy jacks. But would it?

I turned the wheel hard over; as the bow moved across the horizon, heading up into the gale, the sail began to empty and shiver. The bow moved higher, and the sail lost its grip on the wind. It began to flog violently as I began to ease the tension on the halyard, paying out the line, watching carefully as the head of the sail eased away from the mast. I was well aware of the danger of what I was doing: if *Serenity* stopped turning up into the wind and fell with the breeze behind her, the sail would fill again and, with no forward motion, would be unable to withstand the crushing force of the gale without the support of the slackened halyard.

The boat still responded, pushing higher and higher into the wind, leaving me free to lower slowly the furiously whipping canvas.

The great wave broke hard across the starboard bow.

Serenity twisted violently to the left. Falling quickly, flailing impotently on the port side, the wishbone boom wrenched forward. The wind exploded into the empty sail, which hung for an indecisive moment; then up – shivering, full and driving. Balloon-like, the fabric grew taut, then shiny, the sun reflecting red off the glistening concave surface. With a roar that could be heard above the fury of the storm, the sail tore across its full width from luff to leach. The lower portion fell sullenly to the deck as the rest whipped to the top of the mast, wrapping around the spar and halyards, transformed into a horizontal plume challenging the wind almost sixty feet above the water.

All the planning and back-up systems, all my studying and experience would be of little use unless I could retrieve the halyard or raise another sail on my second line, which was fouled in the mess at the masthead, well above my reach.

Most of that night was spent lashing down everything on deck and puzzling over the halyard problem. I caught some fitful snatches of sleep but by sunup I was damp and exhausted, feeling slightly sorry for myself in the closed cabin as the gale assaulted the boat. At times, the cascades of dark green water passing over the deck came so close on each other that the view *out* of the porthole was like looking *in* on some turbulent aquarium.

"There is about twenty days of food onboard," I wrote in my journal, "and enough water to last a month to five weeks. I'm going to check my flares and other distress equipment in case a ship should pass within sight, although I have yet to see one in this part of the Atlantic."

After breakfast of oatmeal and coffee I spent the morning propped in the corner of a bunk, sewing what slides and grommets I could cannibalize from the ruined main into the smaller stormsail, which had been damaged earlier because of the same poor construction. Despite his experience and international reputation the sailmaker back home had produced faulty merchandise. I augmented my survival instincts by

9

planning, in detail, the retribution I would inflict on him upon my return.

Using a sailmaker's palm, needle, and dacron thread, I reinforced the material around the grommets to take the normal strains of sailing. I knew this could be a futile exercise, as I had yet to devise a means of raising the sail. But the sewing was a painstaking, repetitive job that saved me from brooding about my plight. The storm had gone on so long, I couldn't tell my position; the low grey clouds rendered the sextant useless.

I wasn't going to be beaten, I'd come too far! Somehow I would jury-rig a sail; somehow I would stay at the wheel and compass till we reached harbour; somehow. . . .

Until the storm let up I could do very little, so I turned my attention to planning the repairs I would undertake once the wind eased and the seas calmed enough that I could hold myself steady at the mast and on the after deck.

I had lots of time to think. I was about as far as one could get from land anywhere on this earth – about midway between Africa and South America! The nearest island was St. Helena, Napoleon's last exile, some 1,300 miles to the northeast. With the winds blowing steadily from the north and west, it could be ruled out for a boat that had no sail. There was Tristan da Cunha, another British possession, about 750 miles to the southeast. This one was in the right direction, but without the ability to hold a precise course, how could I reach a volcanic pinhead in the sprawling sea?

I fixed some long, looped rope drogues to the port quarter to keep the stern into the wind. Accepting the waves stern-on caused *Serenity* to pitch bow and stern rather than roll side to side. The waves and swells, however, were not moving in an orderly fashion. Running at right angles to each other they would form great mountains of black water that would send *Serenity* into a gyrating frenzy. The motion on board was the worst I'd ever experienced, compounded by the stuffy dampness of a cabin sealed to keep the sea out and the warmth in.

Having had some sleep, I could make a fairly clear-eyed assessment of my situation. I was slightly north of the main shipping route from Rio to Cape Town. Unfortunately, I was being driven south by the wind and the waves at approximately sixty miles per day. Looking through the cabin portholes, I was about five feet above the water; that meant I could see at most 2.6 miles to the horizon, and that only intermittently. A rescue vessel would have to pass within a circle 5.2 miles in diameter for my boat to be seen, an iffy proposition in a four thousand-mile-wide ocean. In these flecked and foaming seas, a blue and white boat with an aluminum mast blended right in, and I imagined a bored lookout, faced with nothing but mile after mile of ocean, missing me completely. My one advantage, ironically, was that damned remnant of sail flapping from the masthead. I calculated that it could be seen eighteen miles away from a ship's bridge. Tonight I would hang a battery-operated strobe light as high in the rigging as I could.

My flares and smoke cartridges had suffered from salt air and I put them into the oven with the pilot light on, to dry out. Lord only knew whether they would work when the time came – and I knew the time would come within the next few hours, at most a day or so. I made an inventory of the clothes and gear that I would take with me if I abandoned *Serenity* and worked out a procedure for the rescue that had to be close at hand. I had to work quickly.

For some unknown reason I wrote a long letter to the yacht's designer, Mark Ellis of Port Credit, Ontario. Re-reading it, I'm struck by how buoyant and polite I remained despite my predicament, acknowledging that my oversights or mistakes by Antiguan workmen, both beyond Mark's control, had caused most of the problems. Still, a man stranded in the middle of the ocean would have been forgiven a little spleen. The letter included a day-by-day schedule of every little thing that had gone wrong, from broken and corroded fittings, bolts that worked loose in the mast, and the electrical system failure, to blocks that didn't allow enough leverage. The letter ended:

"As far as George Hinterhoeller [the St. Catharines builder] is concerned, he has nothing to apologize for whatsoever. With the exception of a few items that appear on the attached list, he has manufactured a superb boat that any builder could be proud of. . . . The attached list should give you some idea of what led up to the situation I am now enjoying. [*Yes, "enjoying" is the word I used*.] If you read carefully, you will see that we all made a small contribution, but we are all human and imperfect."

This was definitely not the old David Philpott speaking. The man who set out on this trip would have found it difficult, if not impossible, to be so generous. The business language could have been dictated from the offices of D.G. Philpott and Associates anytime; but the sentiments were completely out of character. Here I was, on the southerly edge of the shipping lanes, drifting towards the Antarctic ice. Although I felt that rescue was imminent I could, at any moment, pass deeper into that area of the prevailing westerlies, where the weather could become positively frigid. I had no engine, no sails, no electricity, dwindling food, limited water, and no radio; yet I was calmly dictating a letter to the boat's designer eight thousand miles away. I was trying to be generous, fair, and . . . friendly. Extraordinary, for the man I had been.

Little did I know that I would have long days to reflect on how an over-achieving golden boy of real estate development, a man who hated to lose, and rarely did, came to be facing death alone in the desert vastness of the South Atlantic.

As the sun went down on the evening of September 8 I cooked and slowly ate a satisfying meal, leaving the burners on a little longer than usual to maintain the cabin warmth. I hung up my clothes in the hanging locker, got into my pyjamas, slid between the flannelette sheets, and pulled the extra quilt up to my chin to ward off the encroaching evening chill. I slept.

CHAPTER TWO

*D*URING THE TWENTY-SEVEN YEARS OF OUR MAR-
RIAGE, WANDA AND I HAD ALWAYS VACATIONED
together. Back in the 1950s, when every dollar had to be
watched, holidays were a few days or a long weekend at home
or short trips to friends in New York or Montreal. Later I did a
lot of business travelling and was able to take our two children
and Wanda to almost every city in eastern Canada and the
U.S. By the 1960s Wanda and I flew, either on business or for
pleasure, to various cities and resorts on the West Coast and
took one very memorable trip to Halifax and New England.
These trips became an integral part of our lives and, as the
children got older, Wanda and I would find ourselves alone in
New York or San Diego or skiing in Quebec. We travelled
regularly, but for close to a decade we had gone to Delray
Beach, Florida, for a short holiday every spring and fall.

Delray had little to offer except all the creature comforts,
lots of sun and beach, and a reasonable amount of privacy: a
perfect place to unwind from the pressures of business. I
fished and swam, and sunned and relaxed, every year, until
the day in March, 1977, when I decided to substitute a ten-
speed bicycle for a DC-8.

Wanda was in shock when, a week or two before we were to
fly down, I announced that I was leaving the next morning and
would meet her at Delray in about three weeks. I am sure she
didn't believe me until I wheeled the bike out at dawn and
pointed it toward Buffalo.

Ostensibly, the shiny blue ten-speed was for the occasional
trip to the milk store or to pedal down to the yacht club. My
family never got up before nine or ten a.m. on the weekends
and I had become a restless early riser, a habit ingrained by
early flights and business breakfasts. I'd have a quick dip in

the pool, slip into my clothes, and pedal my Centurion to the yacht club for a slap-up breakfast.

It wasn't long before I turned this mundane pastime into a challenge. On weekdays I was up before sunrise, doing ten to twenty miles before coming home for a swim, a shower, and a stand-up breakfast. Every morning my bicycle could be found locked to the chain-link fence around the station where I caught the 8:20 train into Toronto.

I began to strike out early on weekend mornings, pedalling ten, twenty, thirty, eventually sixty miles before breakfast. I'd push myself all the way to the Caledon Hills, using the ski club that I'd helped to build as my destination. It was uphill, but I hardly noticed, exhilarated by whizzing along country roads and sleepy streets creasing the morning mist, savouring the sights and smells of Ontario. Then it was downhill all the way home, and I could push the machine and myself to our limits. I had always been athletic, but cycling developed thighs and hamstrings of steel, and I could pedal by the hour without fading, gliding on the rhythmic pumping of my legs and heart. Best of all, I was alone. Cycling was an escape and an adventure, and I began dimly to understand that this was what I craved.

The challenge had gone out of my work, the only constant in my life. It was still profitable but had become flat and uninspiring. I had "made it," and it wasn't enough.

Compounding these uneasy feelings was my increasing estrangement from my family. I felt that I was always circling warily, and that my children and Wanda were becoming strangers, that all of us were quick to take offence, and often sullen and unreachable.

My decision to undertake my bike safari was made in an instant, but, in reality, it had been coming for months. The kids, who lived at home intermittently, between jobs and spasmodic driftings in and out of university, could not be expected to understand. Although we had enjoyed an intense, loving relationship into their teens, as Stephen and Wendy became adults our interests diverged, and we had been living in separate worlds for ten years. With Wanda, however, it was different. The vitality of our relationship had, if anything, grown and matured with time. This lack of mutual under-

14

standing was relatively recent and I was unwilling to admit openly that anything was seriously amiss.

After one of our frequent tiffs, I took the usual, easy way out, and moved from Mississauga into a Toronto hotel. Around the corner was a Thomas Black & Sons, International Camping outfitter, where I picked up a tent and a sleeping bag, a pair of yellow pannier bags, cycling shorts and shirts, a nylon shell jacket, socks, and the like. During the early months of 1977 I would meticulously list the cycling clothing that was most comfortable at varying temperatures and wind speeds. This gave me firsthand knowledge of the protection I would require on my anticipated trip through the Appalachian Mountains to Florida. Once my decision was made, I postponed my business appointments for the three weeks I thought I'd need, drove home to Mississauga, and confirmed that I was leaving next morning. I promised Wanda I'd call her daily and would meet her in Delray Beach.

I was about to embark on my first solitary voyage.

It was 7:45 a.m. on Thursday, March 24, 1977, a numbing overcast morning, when I set off down Highway 2. I had my American Express card in one cycling shoe, fifty dollars in the other, and some travellers cheques and American currency in a money belt. I settled into a steady, easy pace right away and the anticipation was wonderful.

For twenty years I had been running corporations, and for that and a decade more I'd been a dutiful and ambitious husband and father. This was the first really irresponsible thing I had ever done. There was something beautifully purposeless in the whole enterprise – a tranquil aimlessness in going somewhere without knowing the route I'd take. I would joke later that I'd just gone to Buffalo and turned right.

I'd been thorough to a fault in preparing clothing, camping gear, tools, replacement parts, and physical conditioning; but I'd not planned a route. I bought a cheap road atlas, and pasted on the map of each state I expected to travel through city maps and information clipped out of a Holiday Inn directory. I wrote my health insurance number and my telephone credit card number on the last page and started a log on the cover: miles, departure, arrival, hours, and weather. That was all there was to it.

The first day I was able to write that I arrived at four p.m. in Fort Erie after eight and three-quarters hours of cycling in sunny, pleasant weather, high 27F, low 17F. There was still snow on the margins of the roads, and I wore my cold weather clothes. As it warmed up I would peel them off, one item at a time, and stuff them in the bags. I had twelve and a half pounds of clothing, of which I wore six at the start: street socks, thermal socks, Duo-fold underwear, jockey shorts, slacks, a T-shirt, a heavy Viyella shirt with a wool sweater and nylon jacket. Cotton work gloves, a sailor's watch cap, and hard-soled cycling shoes took care of my extremities. In exceptionally cold or windy weather I could add heavy gloves and a foul-weather jacket. As it warmed up, items of clothing would be transferred from my body to the panniers.

Although I needed the warm clothes, it was essential that they be as light as possible. I'd even cut out labels and weighed clothing alternatives on laboratory scales. I planned to send home, from two or three points on the trip, the clothes that I would no longer need as the weather became warmer. When all that's pushing you is your legs, and the main resistence is weight, every extra ounce counts.

I'd invested in camping equipment but quickly realized that "roughing it" was not for me. I was too tired at the end of a day to set up camp and cook, so it was motels all the way. This allowed me to mail home duplicate clothing, and all my camping gear on the second day out, as I could wash out my underwear and sweat-soaked clothes every night. The reduction in weight made an incredible difference. Much of the tough slogging was now behind me and, although I had mountains to climb for the next thousand miles, I felt like a truck that had been transformed into a sports car.

I couldn't travel on controlled access highways, nor would I have wanted to. The muted solitude of the back roads suited both my method and my mood. No matter what little moose path I was on when I crossed a state line, there was always a kiosk or general store where I could pick up maps and directions; and the ever courteous state or municipal police would always give me the information I needed.

I knew my range was somewhere between sixty and 120 miles a day, certainly nothing more than 160, although I had done more than 200 miles on weekends back home. Each evening, after my long, hot bath, I would circle in different colours destinations on the map sixty, ninety, and 120 miles away. It all depended on the weather and terrain: if the Appalachians perversely decided to be particularly onerous and God provided a headwind, I might put only forty miles behind me. On flat land with a tail wind I could quadruple that comfortably. Each evening I would attempt to anticipate the terrain and wind for the following day, selecting optimum destinations and alternatives in case I had called the shots incorrectly.

I would never cycle much after four p.m., and I'd always start at sunup. If by, say, two p.m., I'd reached my eighty-five-mile goal, I'd press on. If I hadn't reached my new goal by later afternoon, I'd have a sense of accomplishment anyway, having put an extra ten or twelve hours of cycling under my belt, checking into a motel satisfied, sweating gloriously, exhausted but happy!

Nobody travelling to Florida by car would follow the route I took. Unlike those who sit on Interstate 81 holding the pedal down for days, I was constantly making choices: this turn, or that junction, this town or that motel, seeing what I like to think is the real America: the little stores, the rural accents and attitudes, the religious posters in the Bible belt, the old and new headstones in the cemeteries, the raccoons scampering away, the dogs running towards, the dirty sewage and the sweet water, the people. The United States that can't be seen from freeways, where the shoulders of the roads are a white blur, but to me are made up of individual pebbles each with a character and a colour of its own. It was beautiful, a wonderful time of year. Every day the foliage changed, the countryside took on a new personality, and I often had it all to myself for hours and hours, on roads that went up and down like a ribbon nobody over cut.

By my fourth day out, I had removed the winter clothes. At Kitanning, Pennsylvania, I had a late start because of a broken spoke, but I made New Stanton about forty-five miles away by 4:15 p.m. I was enjoying the ride and the solitude and kept pretty much to myself, exchanging only the necessary pleasantries with restaurant and motel staff. The question I always got was "Where are you going?" Nobody seemed interested in the real adventure – where I had started, and how far I had come. I did get a few sidelong glances from motel clerks, which is not surprising, as I was sweat-soaked and probably smelled like a fullback at halftime, and insisted on taking the bike into my room. If any of them thought I wasn't playing with a full deck, they kept the thought to themselves.

Checking into my motel was always one of the high points of the day. How, in my past life, could so mundane an event have been a memorable experience? I now realized that I was on the threshold of new sensitivity, perception, understanding, and appreciation. At the same time I was treating my body as an achievement machine. This was the mind that had built a thirty-year career based on bigger, better, faster, smarter. Keening along those back roads, stretching and pushing my leg and stomach muscles, squeezing out the next mile, over another hill, on to the next town, I was a mechanical thing fuelled by food, lubricated by sleep, driven by ambition.

I ate about every three hours, but my understanding of nutrition was flat out wrong. At a rest stop I'd drink a quart of skim milk and eat a carton of cottage cheese and a banana, all high in protein. Despite my penchant for intense research I'd come up with a completely misguided set of criteria for eating. Although I knew the rudiments of good nutrition for normal living I had not investigated the peculiar needs of a body subjected to extended periods of stress and resultant fatigue. I assumed, since big-league athletes downed huge steaks before a game, lots of protein was the answer. I wound up burning body fat and, eventually, muscle tissue to make up for the carbohydrates and calories I was missing. By the time I reached Florida, I was a skelton, down almost thirty-five pounds from my normal weight of one hundred and seventy-five. (When later I consulted a nutritionist, I found that what I *should* have been doing was drinking whole milk or even cream, eating pasta and chocolate – gobs of calories and food high in carbohydrates.)

The miles rolled past: New Stanton, Pennsylvania, to Morgantown, West Virginia; Morgantown to Elkins, Virginia. For some reason I spent fifteen hours in the saddle between Elkins and Covington, Virginia, killing 113 miles. It was a stupid thing to do, pushing myself so hard, because I had been making remarkably good time and the bicycle had developed a slight but annoying wobble. At Covington I got the offending wheel straightened out and then did a two-day push into North Carolina. The mountains were now all behind me.

My eleventh day out was Sunday, and, as I have an ill-defined yet compulsive attraction to religion and things spiritual, I wandered into a small white-frame church outside Martinsville, Virginia. Being the only white member of the congregation, I was somewhat of an oddity, but after the service, leaning against my bike and chatting to a knot of locals dressed in their Sunday finery, I found myself more than accepted; I received three invitations to family dinners.

Late that afternoon I had my only accident. I had had morbid fantasies about being run off the road by some yahoo or blown away by an eighteen-wheeler or even mugged and robbed (hence the credit card in the shoe); but when I finally took a header it was because I did something stupid even for an inexperienced kid: I got my wheel caught in a railroad track. The bicycle flipped, and I was spread all over the main intersection of High Point, North Carolina. There was blood everywhere: I had ripped up my right leg pretty badly on the asphalt. Purplish, oozing claw marks ran from ankle to hip. Yet none of the people walking the sidewalk offered to help me as I scrambled around, retrieving bits of gear before the heavy, unconcerned traffic crushed it. So much for southern hospitality.

Hurt as I was, and I had no idea how badly, and angry as I was, I carried on for another twenty miles. I had set a certain damned motel as my goal during my previous evening's plotting, and I was determined to get there. Instead of being sensible and finding accommodation in High Point, I doggedly pushed on through squalls of wind and rain with the same illogical determination that had been a major contributor to both my business success and my alienation from my family.

When I got to the motel in Thomasville, North Carolina, I gingerly blotted the grit out of the abrasions on my leg and went to the coffee shop. After my meal I found that I couldn't get out of the chair. My right leg was frozen, bent in the sitting position, as though wrapped in plaster. "Well, this is the end," I thought, but my pigheadedness won out, and I struggled out of the chair, dragged myself to my room, and sank into another hot bath, trying to massage away the pain and stiffness. It didn't do much good. I spent a restless night of fitful sleep punctuated by pain; yet the accident had narrowed and focused my determination. I would not be defeated. Nothing mattered but getting there.

The next morning, dragging a useless right leg and leaning on my bicycle, I pushed my way out of the motel room into the brilliant sunshine, not sure if I could even pedal. Miraculously, the damaged tendons were for walking only. I could ride quite well: the broken parts of the machine had nothing to do with riding, so ride I would. I'd stop at a general store, drag myself in for a cold drink and out again, then pedal off as though nothing were the matter.

I kept it up for six days, through North and South Carolina and Georgia in good, warm weather. I mailed home the last of my heavy clothes and found I could ride without a shirt most days. I crossed into Florida about nine a.m. on Sunday, April 9, seventeen days and almost 1,100 miles out of Toronto.

As I entered Jacksonville, the largest American city in area, I asked a policeman where I could find a hospital. "A block over and two blocks down," he said. My uncanny luck had not deserted me. In this sprawling, unknown city that takes a day to cycle through, I landed up three blocks from the biggest hospital in town. The doctors treated me like a celebrity, and staff kept popping in to meet this guy who'd ridden a bike all the way from Toronto. It did wonders for my ego.

The doctors told me, after x-rays, that aside from some surface abrasions that were healing nicely, I had badly bruised a set of muscles down the side of my right leg. Nothing was torn or broken, and the pain would gradually subside. For a hero, no charge! My pride received as much therapy as my leg, as an admiring coterie of doctors and nurses wished me Godspeed and waved me on to greater adventures.

The next day, on the flat with a tail wind, I made the 101 miles to Daytona in only six and a half hours, and the rest of the ride to Delray was without incident. Head winds slowed me down some, but the sun shone and the warm Florida

20

breeze felt wonderful as I went through Cocoa Beach, Fort Pierce, and Palm Beach. I arrived at the door of the Barrington Hotel, Delray Beach, about one p.m. on my twenty-first day out of Toronto.

I'd covered 1,450 miles: eleven days in mountains, two days soaked by rain; the best day: 113 miles (from Elkins, West Virginia, to Covington); the worst: 40 miles (from Brookfield to Kittaning, Pennsylvania). I'd been cold (12°F one morning in Warren, Pennsylvania) and I'd been hot (88°F in Savannah, Georgia). There had never been a more exhausted, bruised, and sweaty patron at the Barrington, I'm sure. I wheeled the bike into the lobby, grinned at the clerk, and asked if my room was ready. I fell into bed and slept the clock around, contented, happy, and fulfilled.

The next day, I had just surfaced and was trying to blink the sleep out of my eyes when the phone rang. "Hello, Mr. Philpott? This is Barry Bearak of the *Miami Herald* calling. How are you today?" said a cheery voice. I mumbled a rhetorical report on the state of my health and, in a weak moment, agreed to meet the reporter a couple of hours later. The desk clerk had tipped the paper to my arrival, and Bearak had been assigned to do a story on the trip and me. I was a little annoyed: it seemed to cheapen my adventure to have it treated as "human interest" fodder for the newspaper.

I stood under the shower for what seemed like an hour, letting the hot water beat a tattoo on my back and the still-aching muscles of my leg. I even found myself humming – something I never do. Then I stood in front of the full-length mirror and took a hard look at myself for the first time in three weeks. My muscles stood out in sharp relief; they had that "ripped to the bone" definition so prized by body builders, but without the pneumatic, grotesque effect. There wasn't an ounce of fat: I'd consumed most of it by my deficient diet, and the days of hunching over the handlebars had built my forearms until they rippled like a bundle of cables. The sun had bleached and dried my hair the tow colour of my childhood, and it refused to lie down unless slicked with water. My stomach was as flat as an eighteen-year-old's, my face gaunt. Seeing all that thinness made me suddenly ravenous.

I threw on my only long pants and a clean T-shirt, went

21

downstairs, and devoured two plates of bacon and eggs and four cinnamon Danish pastries. Fortified, I called Wanda and told her I'd arrived in one piece. She seemed only marginally interested in my journey but sounded genuinely happy to be coming to join me.

The newspaper interview was pleasant and undemanding, and resulted in a modest story headlined, incorrectly, "He Turned Left At Buffalo." The photographer had got me to climb aboard the bike and pedal around the drive in front of the hotel, and the picture gave a fair impression of how I must have looked, windblown and hard driving, on the road.

When Wanda arrived, we spent a pleasant and relaxing week, fattening me up, sunning, and swimming. It was almost like old times, but with an edge. Wanda seemed to take my trip as a personal affront and, typically, I detoured around the subject rather than confronting it. When we flew back to Toronto, Wanda seemed to assume that I'd had my fling, albeit with a bicycle, and it was finally out of my system.

In Toronto, I went to Mount Sinai Hospital for a second opinion on my leg and treatment for "cyclist's wrist." My right hand had turned into a claw, the outer three fingers locked and immovable. The condition was caused by all those days of carrying approximately one-third of my weight on my hands, crouched over the handlebars, although it appeared only after my arrival in Florida. With massage and heat therapy to the pinched nerve the fingers gradually relaxed, so that after a few weeks I could once again hold a fork and that essential business tool, a pen. The Mount Sinai doctors got me to see a nutritionist, who shook her head at the way I'd eaten, and then set me straight, giving me a diet that would prove to be invaluable.

I knew that I had accomplished something significant: I had tested my ability to achieve alone. With a few exceptions, my past successes had been team efforts. I wasn't utilizing a company of professionals and consultants to conclude a business deal. The experience had not been shared; it – and the joy – had been mine alone. My normal reaction to this feeling would have been one of guilt – it was selfish and self-centred – yet I felt emancipated and confident. I had tasted single-handed accomplishment and the craving would not leave me.

I found during the next few weeks that the telling of my story seemed to bore most women (after the initial "gee-whiz" they drifted away); but it had an odd fascination for men, and they demanded more and more detail, particularly about my feelings and, curiously, my motivation. I remained diffident – talking about it only if asked – and few friends knew that I was planning a bigger challenge: to cycle clear across the country.

Wanda knew, and it soured things. Scarcely a day went by without my taking some heat over it; yet the decision to take the trip brought me a certain peace, as though I had transcended the world of work, family, and responsibility, however temporarily. I attacked each day with unbounded energy but found myself gliding through my workaday life as though trying to become invisible. Always, in the back of my mind, was the memory of that exhilaration and heady freedom on the back roads of Appalachia alone, on a bike.

Early in June, with a stomach full of carbohydrates (I'd learned my lesson), brand new chamois-lined cycling shorts, padded handlebars to avoid "cyclist's wrist," and my credit card back in my shoe, I pedalled north for Thunder Bay. Again, I took along the camping equipment; again, by the time I'd gone 100 miles I realized I was never going to use it and shipped it home. I carried one pair of underwear and one change of socks, which I washed each night in my motel. I rode clean every morning.

The trip to the Lakehead is tough, very steep, cutting through the rocky vastness of the Shield. The wind almost uncannily swung so that it was always in my face. The compensation was that the scenery was breathtakingly beautiful. It is a cliché to say such a thing about the country north of Superior, but out in the open air the effect was heightened. The smell of those piney rocky woods rivals anything on earth. Occasionally, I had to stop, just to take in as much as I could.

The dark side of this beauty is how it is being despoiled. All along the Superior shore, between the sparkling streams, are tributaries turned into stinking sewers by the pulp industry. The slime and algae can be seen building up along the shore line. In only a few years the lake could be dead, one more victim of the unending war between the needs of our environment and those of our economy.

The tidy little motels and hotels that I found in Pennsylvania, Virginia, and the Carolinas were rare in the vastness of northern Ontario. Quite often I would find myself committed to a journey of 150 miles in a day, simply to find accommodation. Sometimes I was limited to only fifty or sixty miles, to avoid a 220-mile push to the next motel.

Because I was up early every morning, I seemed always to start out in fog. Several times timber trucks loaded sideways, the logs jutting beyond the truck bed, came roaring out of the murk and passed within a foot or so of me. Twice, I ducked at the last second and felt the wind of an overhanging log missing my head.

When I reached Thunder Bay, six days out of Toronto, I booked myself a bedroom on the train and loaded my bike into the baggage car. The porter wondered aloud what a guy like me (I think he meant a "bum") was doing with an expensive bike and a first-class bedroom. So I told him. It spread like wildfire through the train: the conductor went on about it and virtually every passenger knew; even the engineer came back to shake my hand. Despite my penchant for anonymity, I got a kick out of being a hero for the two days it took to get back to Toronto.

On the back of a diningcar placemat, with a map spread out in front of me, I sketched a plan to cover the rest of the country except for Newfoundland and Prince Edward Island. I would do it in stages, so I could continue running a business while indulging in this trip of a lifetime. I established the continental divide at Lake Louise, from where, in theory at least, it would be downhill both to Vancouver and back to the Lakehead. To the east, it was simple: take the Trans-Canada highway from Toronto until I reached the sea.

By the end of the first week in July, I had tidied up my affairs sufficiently to squeeze out a ten-day ride to the East Coast. At dawn on July 8, I struck out from Mississauga. Wanda stood at the door impassively.

The eastern leg was uneventful. Some rain and headwinds dogged my passage, and the heat got to me; but I enjoyed a generally quiet and contemplative ride. Quebec City has always been a favourite of mine; it is Canada's most beautiful and friendly city, and it was there I crossed the St. Lawrence on the Lévis ferry and took the road to Rivière-du-Loup before turning south. (A year or so later I would be crossing that same ferry route on *Serenity IV*, also destined for the Atlantic.) I arrived in Saint John in the mid-afternoon on July 17, having made 100 miles a day on average. I rode until I found a beach on the Bay of Fundy; I walked my bike into the slowly lapping surf, a symbolic demarcation of one end of my route, and flew home.

I celebrated my fiftieth birthday by putting my business affairs in order and overhauling my faithful bicycle. I flew to Calgary on August 11, took a bus to Lake Louise, and started "downhill" to Vancouver. Eastern town names – Kingston, Brockville, Cornwall, Lachine, Joliette, Trois-Rivières, Rivière-du-Loup, Fredericton – are the old Canada, steeped in hundreds of years of history. In the West, the names speak of adventure, pioneering, and the opening up of a new land. Golden, Beavermouth, Revelstoke, Kamloops, Squamish – the new Canada, waiting to be discovered.

From the Continental Divide to the Pacific the giant mountains and arrid valleys would give way within a day to fertile river basins producing two crops a year. I had skied the mountains and done business in the cities; but I had never really seen this country as I did on that 11,000-foot drop from Lake Louise to Vancouver.

Although the trend was down, there were many muscle-testing uphill stretches to contend with, and to add to the difficulties, I'd miscalculated the sunrise. I'd forgotten the shading effect of mountains and found myself riding in the pitch dark for two early morning hours. I went through Golden, B.C., without even seeing it. And at one point something with hooves clattered across the road a bicycle-length ahead of me.

The first major challenge was Rogers Pass at the heart of Glacier National Park. For hours, in low gear, my progress was excruciatingly slow; I had to concentrate so hard on driving the bike forward that I saw little on the way up. I was dehydrating because of the heat and the exertion required for mountain riding, and I developed a prodigious thirst, an on-going craving that I hadn't encountered on my Florida trip. The general stores and watering spots were scarcer than I had expected.

I reached the summit of the Pass after eleven hours of climbing at a greater than six per cent grade. By late afternoon I sprawled on my back in the bracing waters of a mountain stream to summon the strength to make it to Revelstoke. I covered 142 miles that day, and it was too much. God arranged a sand-filled headwind escort for my last forty miles.

Despite my resolve to husband my strength, I put in another thirteen hours the next day, from Revelstoke to Kamloops. I've never known fatigue like it; it was as though the juices had been sucked out of me. I soaked in the tub and drank two quarts of water. I wasn't hungry but craved liquids: I had ignored the 102°F heat, further proof that I learn most of my lessons the hard way.

My third day out, I covered a measly fifty-two miles, but they were hard won. The hills were smaller, but came one after another after another. Again there was a prevailing head-wind; and the soaring cedars, glacial streams, and majestic railway tunnels of my previous day's scenery had given way to an arrid, desert-like land. The last fifteen miles were agony, and I quit at Cache Creek about noon. I slept the afternoon away, and most of the night. I tried to eat some carbohydrates. I was becoming a banana junkie – they were good for me and easy to eat – but other food just didn't interest me.

I was just over two hundred miles from Vancouver, and the highway was becoming easier. On August 15, during the two hours before the sun peeked over the mountains, I covered twenty-four miles; by day's end, in 100°F heat, I'd put 105 miles behind me to reach Yale, B.C.

I was up early the next day, knowing that, with luck, I could reach Vancouver that afternoon. The morning started beautifully, but by eleven a.m. the heat was getting me down. Once in the Vancouver suburbs, traffic and my rear tire became problems. I kept pumping up the tire, which had developed a slow leak, and by sheer luck I found a bike shop to repair it.

I arrived at the Vancouver CPR station at 3:45 p.m., wheeled up to the counter, and reserved a bedroom back to Lake

Louise. By ten p.m. I was asleep on my way back to the summit. The next day I off-loaded the bike and headed down to Banff, a two-hour ride. I was in a glorious frame of mind. I'd met several people on the train, all of whom had confirmed my view that my trek was worthwhile. A seventy-year-old, swore he'd have gone along if he were forty years younger!

From Banff, I virtually coasted downhill into Calgary, covering eighty-one miles by noon. I phoned Toronto, Sarnia, New York, and other places where I'd been consulting on urban development, and I met with some lawyers in my hotel. I was dressed in my cycling clothes; but they knew what to expect.

I called Wanda.

I left the hotel in cold weather gear. It was 27°F; but there was no wind, so the slightly hilly country east of Calgary was an easy run. There wasn't much to look at, the land kept monotonously productive by rigorous irrigation. It was on stretches like this my mind drifted: snatches of music, nonsense tunes (often rhythmically linked to the cadence of the pedals), or images of sailing and soft-focus cameos of childhood.

My memory moved gently through pictures of the past. Scarsdale, north of New York City, where I was born: my father digging a hole for a small lamp post. The post fell on him and cut his head slightly. I was frightened; I was about three years old. Our house in Toronto: it had eighteen rooms, a six-car garage, and servants. That was before my father lost his fortune. We had just heard on the radio that the Germans had invaded Poland and we were at war. I started a diary, which recorded three days of history, when the writer lost interest.

My one-bedroom home on Toronto Island; my children, Stephen and Wendy: they used to cuddle and smell nice. Happy, loving family dinners at Christmas and birthdays at the house in Mississauga; Wanda's touch and smile, her reassuring words. Coaching Stephen's hockey team; field days and garden parties at Wendy's school.

I was in love, with my wife and my family, and they were in love with me. I could shut out everything unpleasant.

On my fourth day, I left Brooks, Alberta, about 7:15 a.m. I

27

was losing my mania for pre-dawn starts, and this would be my first flatland run. I did my fastest stretch ever – from Brooks to Medicine Hat in four and a half hours – averaging fifteen mph with a couple of stops.

I was on the dead level Trans-Canada, parallel to the CPR and the traffic was light. The occasional pickup whooshed by, shrinking in the distance until it disappeared over the horizon. I was just west of Suffield, Alberta, Canada's germ and chemical warfare research establishment, when a dusty, battered green Pontiac pulled beside me, slowed up ahead, and stopped. A big, bearded guy got out. This was it: I was about to be mugged in the middle of nowhere, and I was defenceless.

It was Stephen. I knew my son had been working at Fort McMurray, getting big money for working long hours, where there's nowhere to spend it. Most people can't take it for more than a few months, and Stephen had reached his limit and was heading east. He didn't even know I was riding across the country.

We sat in his car on the soft shoulder and chatted stiffly, as only a father and twenty-seven-year-old son can. It had probably been a year since we had talked face-to-face, yet, we'd been close, Stephen and I, in the early years. We are different men, and when Stephen contracted the disease of adulthood our differences grew into estrangement. I felt that he was judging me.

I watched the transcontinental passenger train crawl from one horizon to the other while exchanging banalities with a very straight, programmed, compliant kid. Maybe that was my fault. I always gave the impression, however unsubstantiated, of being powerful and dominant during his childhood. Right or wrong, I always avoided forcing him to stand up to me; and he never did rebel. I knew he could never win in a confrontation, so I seemed to be forever backing away. It's not unreasonable that he'd think I was disinterested, that I didn't love him.

As I got out of the car, Stephen seemed to offer some frail hope for reconciliation: he was going to Kenora to look for work and invited me to call on him on my way through. When I got to Kenora I asked every marina and resort operator in town about Stephen, but no one knew his whereabouts. I hear news of him, but I haven't seen him since.

I found the going difficult the rest of that day and the next. Perhaps it was my morale had been broken in my encounter with Stephen; perhaps it was the steady rain and a wicked lateral wind that let me go only eighty-one miles. But I was at the halfway point, and the trip had to be completed.

The cold seeped into my bones, although I wore every piece of cold weather clothing I had. I was starting out early again, at 4:15 a.m., largely because I seemed to sleep fitfully and woke well before dawn. I covered 112 miles, from Swift Current to Moose Jaw; and the next day, 107 miles to Wolseley, Saskatchewan, against a real grass-bender headwind.

The wind increased the next day, and I ground out the seventy-five miles to Moosomin, Saskatchewan, in low gear or one up. I talked with Wanda that night and came away in a better frame of mind. Maybe I was learning something. The following day I rode a tailwind all the way to Portage la Prairie, Manitoba, 165 miles away.

During the next few days I again began to lose my resolve. I felt depressed by the dreary country, the Scotch mist, and the punishing wind. I bypassed Winnipeg and, by mid-afternoon of August 27, I'd reached Willard Lake, Ontario, just east of Kenora, where I'd tried to find Stephen. I was ready for the trip to end. The rain played tag with the sun, alternately soaking and warming me; I just kept my head down and pumped. If I had once fancied myself a machine, becoming one was now the only way to finish. I was constantly chilled, and the roads were treacherous.

Around Upsala, with Shabaqua and the end in sight, I began to perk up. I phoned Wanda, who seemed amiable, even eager to see me home. My final miles were joy.

It wasn't until I had checked in my bike and sat in the Thunder Bay airport departure lounge waiting for a flight to Toronto that it really came to me: I had done it. From sea to sea. I felt good, but not as good as I had expected to feel. Tired and drained as I was, I felt restless and incomplete. Something remained to be done.

CHAPTER THREE

I'*D NEVER HANDLED A BOAT ON SALT WATER, BUT THE NOTION OF A LONG BLUE-WATER SAILING VOYAGE HAD* been in the back of my mind since I was child. From the first days of sailing our old twenty-five-foot *Canuck*, and then my cruising sloop *Wanwind*, discovering the pleasures of my own company on long, bracing lake trips, what had been a fantasy was becoming a resolve. Almost every serious sailor of a sea-kindly yacht has suffered from the itch to pit himself against the elements, to test himself on the open ocean. Yet few actually plan such a venture, and even fewer realize the ambition. It's really no different from the driver of a six-year-old Datsun dreaming about being on the Paul Newman racing team, or the jogger musing about running the Boston Marathon.

My daydreams started out as insubstantial as theirs. Certainly I didn't begin with the idea of sailing solo around the world; the idea was neither that grand nor that specific at first. It was a simple but recurring image of being at the wheel of a yacht, knifing majestically through crisp blue waters, a fanciful quixotic, even menopausal vision. With most of us, it goes no farther than musing, but I had just put 5,000 miles of adventurous cycling behind me, and that energetic and eccentric experience had swept away a lot of inhibitions. Cycling had liberated the romantic in me. Far from exhausting my appetite for solitude, challenge, and adventure, the bike trips had whetted it. That my marriage was in serious trouble, and that much of the problem lay with me, was not enough to quell this fit of liberation. My mental picture of the ocean voyage had taken on fresh and vibrant colours as I completed the last leg of the cross-Canada trip. When I symbolically dipped my front wheel in the Bay of Fundy and the Burrard Inlet, the blue-water cruise left the realm of fantasy.

30

I'd had opportunities for ocean sailing, of course, but I had always deflected the urgings of business friends in Vancouver, Halifax, and San Diego. The idea must have been, from the beginning, to do it *myself*.

For years I had been reading about small boat ocean sailing, from H.A. Callahan in the early days to Naomi James. Thor Heyerdahl's account of *Kon-Tiki's* voyage across the Pacific in 1947 was one of many describing exotic ocean ventures, the most notable being Francis Chichester's solo circumnavigation in 1967 and Joshua Slocum's in the 1890s. When Chichester set sail from Plymouth on August 27, 1966, he had already established his individuality not only as a sailor but as a pioneer of long-distance solo flying. The parallels between an aeroplane and a bicycle were not lost on me.

Joshua Slocum, however, sailing single-handed, had none of the self-steering and navigational equipment and strong lightweight gear and winches used by modern yachtsmen. Slocum's voyage had been a fairly leisurely, though very adventurous cruise, with plenty of stops between 1895 and 1898. He had avoided Chichester's empty storm-ridden Southern Ocean, rounding the tip of South America east to west through the Straits of Magellan. He was a Nova Scotia-born New Englander in his early fifties who achieved the enviable distinction of becoming the first man to sail around the world alone. Indeed, that is what he called his book: *Sailing Alone Around the World*. It was published in 1900, yet even with its occasionally florid language, it was a powerful motivator for me. A comparison between our voyages is impossible, yet the key elements – sail, wind, solitude, and self-reliance – remain immutable.

Merchant marine officer Robin Knox-Johnson was not even an experienced small-craft sailor when he decided to sail nonstop from Capetown to Gravesend, inspired by Chichester, possibly motivated by a recently broken marriage, and challenged by at least five other sailors. His story and others relating to transatlantic racing, attempts to round Cape Horn, pitch poling in the Bass Straits off Australia, and other detailed accounts of the ocean and its puny challengers added to my vicarious experience. Naomi James was the last single-handed sailor and her book was the first of many I purchased to supplement the library that accompanied me on my voyage.

One of my sailing-related interests is celestial navigation. I had taken courses in it with the Power Squadron and, never one to do anything by halves, taught it at a local community college. Celestial navigation is an ancient and fascinating science; its basic instruments are the sextant and an accurate timepiece. The observer uses the sextant to measure an angle between a celestial body (sun, moon, star, or planet) and the horizon, and records the exact time. After some reasonably complex arithmetic, usually referred to as "reducing the sight," one can establish within five to ten miles one's precise location on the surface of the globe. Now, when that position is a Florida beach or a concrete jetty in Port Credit, navigation is relatively simple. It didn't take much common sense to realize that the same procedure, when executed from the careening deck of a small boat in heavy seas, was quite different. In an odd way, my students fertilized the idea of my ocean voyage. I was amazed at those who didn't do very well on the course, notwithstanding my flawless tuition, who would send me postcards from the Canary Islands or the South Pacific to which they'd sailed using the knowledge of navigation they had gleaned from my classes. If them, why not me? I knew that, compared to a relatively placid trip down the Intercoastal Waterways and through the Panama Canal, an Atlantic crossing, particularly single-handed, was hazardous. But I kept thinking "Why not me?"

My company was running comfortably, but predictably. My assistant, Joan Hammell, had developed a natural talent for my business and could handle the day-to-day finances, field the demands of my clients and customers during my long absences, and make certain that the company performed successfully and efficiently. The mortgage market had been crushed flat by inflation and rate increases. It seemed to be a good time to take to the open sea.

My friend Mark Ellis is both a keen sailor and a highly respected yacht designer. He had a new cutter coming on the market, the Niagara 35, being built by George Hinterhoeller, one of the founders of C & C Yachts and the designer of the Shark. The Niagara 35 was to be the first new yacht to come from Hinterhoeller since he left C & C and struck out on his own.

The yacht was very similar to *Wanwind* – the boat I had owned before the bicycle – but larger and sturdier. It was built to handle off-shore sailing, although I intimated that, some day, maybe, I'd take the boat to sea. Fitted out the way I wanted it, with the simplest electronics, sturdier rigging, and perhaps a single side band radio, the boat was going to suit me perfectly. Hinterhoeller would begin work that fall and I could take possession the following spring.

But it wasn't long after I plunked down my $5,000 deposit that I took a fateful sail with the late Gordon Fisher, president of Southam, Inc. and an avid sailor. He had commissioned Mark Ellis to design a catboat dubbed a Nonsuch. Fisher's boat came off the Hinterhoeller line almost handmade in the summer of 1978, and he took me out for a spin.

To the untutored observer, the Nonsuch is an unlikely looking vessel to elicit love at first sight. It was inspired by the old Cape Cod-style single-sailed working boats, the plump, friendly craft frequently used as cruising boats eighty years ago. Dinghy-shaped underwater, it has plumb ends, that is, it drops straight to the waterline. This means the thirty-footer has space below usually found in boats five or ten feet longer. The interior design was a superb combination of comfort and function.

It has an unsupported mast – there are no stays or shrouds – and no headsail or jib, just one 540-square-foot mainsail that could be reefed and handled easily by one person from the cockpit. The wishbone boom is easier to operate than to describe; but it is, basically, two pieces of aluminum, bowed apart and joined at the ends, straddling the mast. With loose lines joining the two sides, it forms a perfect cradle for the descending sail.

The boat looked vulnerable and incomplete without standing rigging, but it could overtake almost any comparable sized boat on the lake. It was also very forgiving and would sail beautifully even when the sail was casually trimmed.

In the usual sloop rig, shortening sail, that is, reducing the area of canvas exposed to the wind, involves two separate and sometimes difficult operations. The first is the reefing the main, dropping the mainsail a few feet down the mast and gathering the excess material around the boom. The second is replacing the headsail or jib. This headsail is quite often substantially larger than the mainsail and when it has to be dropped in a high wind and perverse sea, a lone sailor may be fighting 500 or 600 square feet of wind-whipped Dacron on a tiny forward deck that is rising and falling through an arc of up to thirty feet.

All my single-handed sailing role models seemed to be forever taking down the number one headsail, replacing it with a number two, removing it a few hours later to put up a Spitfire – all the time endangering their lives and suffering untold discomfort. Chichester, aboard *Gypsy Moth IV*, would be dealing with headsails up on deck in the dark of night as the bow buried itself in coal-black and icy waves. Naomi James and other sailor-authors, too, seemed to be forever crawling to and from the forward deck, wet and cold. The Nonsuch solved the problem by eliminating the headsail. Never once would I go to the forward deck other than to enjoy the calm evening or the warmth of the sun. All reefing could be handled from the cockpit.

The second nightmare of the single-handed sailor is rigging failure. A typical sloop has its mast supported by stainless steel cables held in place on the mast by at least six tangs and two spreaders, and on the hull by as many chainplates and turnbuckles. All of these are vulnerable; each fail, usually in a way that is difficult to repair, at an awkward time and with dispiriting frequency. Almost every authority has at least one horror story of clinging to a mast thirty or forty feet above the deck, trying to notch a shroud on a spreader or to refasten a tang while describing a 60° arc over the raging sea.

The Nonsuch mast was shroud-free: no spreaders, no tangs, no chainplates, no turnbuckles. The mast Ellis designed was really a slightly modified, standard issue aluminum light standard, the type seen along the expressways, designed to hold great fluorescent lamps aloft in all weather. The walls of the mast are one-eighth of an inch thick; it is stepped right down on the keel and seated in a substantial sleeve of reinforced fibreglass plastic. It passes up through the deck, which is reinforced by a massive beam running athwartships, then soars fifty-four feet up, unsupported and secure. Because the force of the sail is distributed over the full height, the mast is able to absorb virtually any wind force: the sail would burst before the walls of the tube could buckle. I had some concern that the whipping of the mast would result in metal fatigue; but there was very little movement as long as the sail was up, and as the sail would be up almost all the time on the ocean, the whipping would be minimal.

Now the last piece of technical data: because it is angled downward from the point where it straddles the mast, the wishbone (which is similar to the boom on a wind sailing board) balances the tension along the edges of the sail and eliminates the need for a boom vang, the line attached to a conventional boom to keep it from riding up with the pressure of wind on the sail.

Only a couple of weeks after my first sail with Gordon Fisher I transferred my order from a Niagara 35 to a Nonsuch and waited impatiently for it, the eighth to roll off Hinterhoeller's line.

All Hinterhoeller knew was that I expected to make a transatlantic crossing sometime in the future. The idea of circumnavigating the world had yet to come. My closest friends and the boat builders understood my desire to sail the open ocean, although they thought single-handed was a bit risky.

I gave the construction of my boat minute scrutiny, spending as much time as possible at the St. Catharines yard. I wasn't a stranger to fibreglass boat-building. For fifteen or twenty years I had visited and poked about in almost every boatyard in Canada, from the Spencer Yards in Vancouver to little one-man operations in weather-beaten sheds on Nova Scotia's south shore. I had even contemplated starting a yacht manufacturing company as a diversion of D.G. Philpott and Associates; there was a slim file on my desk labelled "Yacht Division."

Hinterhoeller's men were fine craftsmen. I am sure I irritated them from time to time with my fussing and changes, and the carpenters blanched when I arrived on one of my regular visits; but the result was exceptional, and the first-class finish was a credit to men who took pride in their work.

Fortunately, I did not have to sacrifice appearance or comfort, but the integrity of the structure was my prime concern;

and I received all the co-operation I needed. I had the yard install heavier than standard wiring throughout the boat, and provision was made for three extra storage batteries. A multitude of minor design changes were incorporated, all spawned by my prodigious research and focused on one thing – the open sea.

I finally took delivery of *Serenity* one bright spring day in 1979. I drove up to the dock at Bronte with Mark Ellis and there, gleaming in the sunshine, she bobbed at anchor. *Serenity IV* was boldly displayed on her stern, and in smaller letters below "Toronto," denoting the hailport. I had chosen the name because of my fondness for the simplicity and wisdom of Reinhold Niebuhr's serenity prayer: "O God, give us serenity to accept what cannot be changed, courage to change what should be changed, and wisdom to distinguish the one from the other." It was an appropriate prescription for the traumatic changes my life was undergoing.

After a shakedown sail from Bronte to Port Credit with Mark Ellis's partner, John Burn, showing me the ropes, I moored at the yacht club and immediately moved aboard. That very evening I sat in the cockpit, bundled up against a bracing spring wind, the lights from the cabin glowing up through the companionway, glinting off shining hardware and varnished teak. Before me stretched the clean uncluttered deck that was to be the hub of my world. The cabin trunk glistened with the night dew, and puddles of yellow light spilled on the deck through the seven large portholes fitted with three-eighth-inch perspex to stand up to any sea. The mast bent ever so slightly before the breeze, giving off a clear, high, clinking as the halyards inside slapped the metal. I'd never known that such contentment could contain the thrill of an adventure yet to start.

Three-quarters of a mile from home, I set up housekeeping aboard *Serenity*. Wanda and I had not yet officially separated but I'd been staying at the Royal York almost continuously. I went home frequently to get new clothes, to have a swim, and to see if there was any mail from the children. After picking up some tools, cooking utensils, or other odds and ends I would slip aboard my new home. It all made a certain sad sense.

Marriages don't break up so much as slowly dissolve, or at

36

least mine did; and it was only during the last few years that there was nothing left. Well into our forties we skied regularly at Caledon, took extensive vacations, with or without the children, and lived the good life. Wanda and I were in love, everyone would see that; appearing to be in love was the social requirement of our day and station. Behind this facade, however, as I expect exists with many couples married twenty years, there was developing a repetitive ritual of living born of tradition, not desire.

I was caught on a rutted straight road that, no matter how pleasant and rewarding, was leading straight to death. In thirty or forty years I was going to die, the same man as I was in 1970. I was the perfect, highly polished casting from the social mould of the 1940s and 1950s, highly programmed with rigid parameters, unquestioned discipline, and an insatiable drive for success. One married for life, loved one's children, and served one's country and community, all without query or doubt.

The day I married I entered into a contract that committed me, unequivocally, to being in love forever. I loved my children, anyone could see that: they had attended private schools since they were twelve years old; they had music, sailing, and skiing lessons; their table manners were impeccable; and Wanda and I were told constantly that we should be proud of such fine young people who had not resorted to drugs, demonstrations, and free love. And, yes, I was a model citizen. I had worked for the church, albeit years ago, managed a little league hockey team, worked for the United Appeal, donated to worthy causes, paid my accounts before the due date, spoke to the Rotary Club, lectured at the university, and taught at the Power Squadron. An all-round dependable fellow!

Dull, dull, dull.

Then the paragon of the 1940s began to crumble. My children saw only an old fart whose knowledge was diminishing month by month; besides, they could ski better than I could. The Home and School Association, service clubs, and church were doing fine without me. I began to withdraw into a solitude that was the beginning of the end. Monday night football with two or three glasses of Scotch became the highlight of my week.

More to placate Wanda than to heal my ailing marriage, I

visited a string of marriage counsellors and psychiatrists. Each said nothing was wrong but insisted on sending me to a greater guru one step higher on the psychiatric ladder. Yet, clearly, I had changed, and since change was not part of the 1940s formula of life, something must be wrong with me. But I was sufficiently docile and obtuse to allow myself to continue this attempt at therapy for more than two years, to no avail.

In order to shake things up a little, we moved to a large house on the lakeshore in Oakville. It was a beautiful property, but too far from the city and, with our children away, too large. A year or so later I sold it and we moved back to Mississauga.

I attacked the remodelling of this latest house with a vengeance: possibly I was attempting to bring back happier times, the year I took to build our bridal cottage on Toronto Island. A carpenter and I tore out the insides of the 4,000-square-foot split-level home on the Credit River and rebuilt it. I revelled in the carpentry, the electrical work, the plumbing – all the trades that I had learned in my youth – after a day at the office and on into the early hours of the morning. Wanda lived at the Royal York Hotel until I could provide civilized accommodation. I lived alone in a little room in the lower level. We were living apart, I was deeply involved in a project of my own creation, and I was enjoying every minute of it.

When Wanda returned, she took over the decorating. I resented sharing my project, the very justification of my life during the previous few months.

It was inevitable: I packed my bags and checked into the Royal York, where I made my home intermittently for the next two or three years. Until I found *Serenity*.

When I look back there was no turning point, no crisis that could be identified as the significant factor. We had lived according to all the rules for twenty years and we believed ourselves to be happy.

I believe that thinking adults cannot sustain happiness and retain their ability to question, learn, and expand their horizons. Ecstasy comes in spasms, like sneezes. Below that there is joy one can experience on occasions. Happiness pokes its way in and out of our lives; it is a state of mind, which for reasons unknown, we chose to reject. The love which we had contracted on our wedding day had eroded. We wanted to end the marriage, so it ended.

Living on *Serenity* was hardly roughing it. Broad and deep, she had plenty of head room and all the necessary comforts. *Serenity* was designed to sleep four, two in quarter berths, half under the cockpit. I used one of these to store my extra sails, and in the compartments adjoining it, I stored the many charts for the trip to the sea. Forward of the galley and the head was the bed that I used, almost three-quarter in size and big enough to sprawl on diagonally. Although *Serenity* was my home, I used the yacht club facilities, even though I had a first-class galley, shower, and washroom on board. It was not that I minded the relatively cramped quarters, but I was saving onboard propane and fresh water, which had to be replenished from time to time, usually not at my convenience. I also disliked cooking and usually ate a hearty business lunch. Only if I was too late to eat at the club did I cook.

One of my first projects aboard was to upgrade the electrical capacity. I purchased three additional batteries and installed them in parallel with the existing units. This gave me a tremendous reserve, which would allow me to go for days without having to charge the batteries at sea. This would save fuel for the main purpose of the engine – carrying me in and out of confined St. Lawrence River ports and down the Maritime coast. At dockside, umbilically connected to the yacht club, I had electric refrigeration, radio, and television.

Everybody at the club was curious about this boat and would detour to peer at her. To the casual observer and to many trained and experienced sailors she was rather clumsy looking, with a broad beam and only thirty feet long, and gave the impression that she might not respond well to the wind and helm. During those first months, however, my original assessment of her appearance and sea-kindliness was reinforced over and over again. But I knew she was beautiful, and also knew that I was going to head out to the Atlantic. I had no precise plans beyond Halifax, but sail out into the Atlantic I must.

I was determined to keep the gadgetry to a minimum, to

make absolutely certain that every system and piece of equipment onboard was backed up; and to know precisely what was needed to repair virtually anything and to stay alive. There was no structural, rigging, mechanical, or electrical system that I didn't modify slightly. Where a back-up was necessary, I installed one, where practicable, in the likely event of failure. I secured to the transom my wind-activated self-steering device, which I later dubbed "George," after the old English movie, *Let George Do It.* I tested it again and again in Lake Ontario during those hot summer months.

I doubled or tripled up almost all my equipment, laying aboard two sextants, twin sets of tools and piloting instruments, extra pairs of reading glasses, and as many substitute parts as I could reasonably carry. On the trip to Halifax I carried just one large mainsail, hoping to learn a bit more about sea conditions before I ordered additional canvas. I would never be far from shore and could motor to any port on the St. Lawrence or Nova Scotia coast. I had a Loran C electronic navigation device aboard, an afterthought purchased at half price at the Toronto Boat Show. I never had great faith in it; it was really a back-up to the sextants. I had two anchors, a life raft, a huge kit of the usual tools including a hand saw and bolt cutters, sailing mending equipment, and small plastic tubs full of extra hardware: bolts and shackles and cotter pins. Most of my spare time was spent haunting the shops or installing or improving some system, machinery, or rigging.

Because I was unsure where my trip would take me I picked up charts for almost every coastline I could conceivably touch. First, across the Atlantic to the Azores, up the European coast to England. Then the African coast, and the eastern coast of South America, then charts for all the Caribbean islands. I also collected sailing directions describing landfalls in minute detail, keyed to the official charts, from the coast of Ireland to Portugal. As well, I bought books written by touring sailors who concentrated on the nitty-gritty of where to get your laundry done and what restaurants were good in Montserrat. This compulsive collecting of information for both sides of the Atlantic was indicative of my unwillingness or inability to plan my life beyond my arrival at Halifax. It wasn't just my route that was in limbo, it was my whole future.

Two fellow sailors at the club had recently taken the Halifax-to-Bermuda run, and I pumped them for all the information I could get. One, whose boat was moored just down from *Serenity* and was slightly larger than mine, had been caught in a terrible storm and had been rescued literally gibbering with fear and shock. He told his story without self-consciousness or shame; he did not have to apologize for his respect for the great Atlantic. The other had tried the run in an Alberg 30, somewhat smaller than the Nonsuch, and had a very rough ride. Hearing their stories confirmed my determination to prepare my boat and to condition myself to win.

Win I knew not what, but failing had no place in the plan. I familiarized myself with *Serenity*, strengthening and rechecking, learning all her whims and idiosyncrasies by sailing her for hours alone under all conceivable weather conditions.

By August 14 I was ready to make the inland leg of my journey, down the Seaway and through the Gulf of the St. Lawrence to Halifax. That last morning was taken up with mundane chores: grocery shopping, storing my car, and picking up the minor items remaining on my checklist.

Joan Hammell could administer my business while I was away. The children were away from home, involved in their own lives, unaware of my departure. Wanda appeared disinterested. She knew where I was going and when I expected to arrive.

The sun was as bright, the air as clear, and my mood as buoyant as the day I had left on my bicycle some eighteen months before on a solitary adventure. I cleared the Port Credit light at 1220 hours, in a brisk thirty-knot wind. It was later than I had planned, and I was mildly concerned that I might not reach Cobourg, the natural stop for my first night out. But *Serenity* seemed as eager as I to be on our way. The waves were running on the starboard quarter at about six feet as I rocketed around Gibraltar point south of Toronto harbour's western gap.

Serenity and I had left our home port without so much as a good-bye to anyone.

CHAPTER FOUR

WHEN THE SQUALL HIT, WE WERE STILL A COUPLE OF HOURS SHORT OF ÎLE AUX COUDRES, A LUMPISH island that lies just off the north shore of the river near Baie St. Paul, where we planned to anchor for the night. The rain was so thick I could hardly breathe, and I was certain we'd soon be aground, blown downwind into one of the many shoals of the St. Lawrence. As I moved forward to let go the anchor John lowered the sail. For an instant, in the grey squall, it could have been Stephen dropping the writhing dacron into the lazy-jacks.

Actually, John Barker and Stephen were poles apart in all but age and appearance, but they had been best friends since they played for the peewee hockey team I coached. Now, at twenty-eight, John was onboard *Serenity*, studying for his bar exams, and Stephen was out there, somewhere, searching still. For that fraction of a second I couldn't help wishing that it was my son instead of John who had shared the past two weeks with me.

Serenity tugged irritably at her anchor. It was only after the third or fourth wind-shipped wave smashed the weather side and laid a sheet of water over the cockpit that I realized I was tasting the salt of the sea! We'd been in tidewater since above Quebec City; the ocean water muscled up the Gulf of St. Lawrence, pushing back the fresh water trying to flow downstream. But now, the river was ending, where the ocean began. The short-lived squall blew itself out, exposing vague outlines of the shoreline and the island ahead. In a misty drizzle, I fired up the diesel and, at dusk, we nosed *Serenity* into a sheltered cove on the south side of Île aux Coudres.

Stripping off his foul-weather gear, John went below; in the half hour it took me to secure the gear for the night and set the anchor, he whipped up some curried chicken, rice, and chappatis, a legacy of John's extensive touring in the East. I could have existed on bread and peanut butter; but it was delightful to have aboard both company and an accomplished cook. If only he didn't dirty every pot, pan, and dish in the galley!

I had picked up John at the Kingston marina two weeks earlier, three days out of Port Credit. All small craft are required to have at least two crew members to traverse the locks of the Seaway, so John was to be my extra hand. He intended to disembark at Quebec City, but by the time we got there he had become addicted and was providing such fine meals that I readily agreed that he stay aboard until Halifax. There would be time enough for solitude once I struck off into the Atlantic.

Although almost twenty-five years my junior, John was wonderful company. He and I had always had a special relationship. Somehow John always made it a point to visit me and talk, even through law school; and we had an easy meeting of minds that had eluded me with Stephen. Without the emotional baggage of a blood tie, John and I developed an adult relationship that eludes many a parent and child.

My trip to Kingston had been uneventful after the first day, which was a glorious start to the journey. *Serenity* covered thirty miles in four hours, making twelve knots at times, some three and a half knots above her hull speed.

It took six days to go from Kingston through the locks to Quebec City. Our progress, mostly under power, was slow because commercial vessels take precedence on what is, after all, a commercial highway. But John kept me amused, engaging the predominantly East Indian seamen on the giant freighters in conversation, using a blend of halting Hindi and pidgin English. A couple of times he even invited them aboard for some "home" cooking; we were running a drop-in centre for lonely sailors.

By contrast, most of the private yachtsmen kept pretty much to themselves; a nod and a wave, a brief exchange of pleasantries was usually the extent of it. However, one fine-looking thirty-five-footer out of Trois-Rivières moored alongside us at the Snell Locks, and I chatted with the owner. I had been unable to acquire the tide tables for the westerly section of the Gulf of St. Lawrence before leaving Toronto, but my new friend kindly gave me his copy of these essential numbers. We started our engines at two a.m. and moved through the canal into the locks, one of the many on our way to Montreal.

I had met many sailors who had cruised to Montreal; indeed, it was the rare yachtsman who hadn't at least tried to sail to Montreal for Expo in 1967. But I knew no one who had gone through the St. Lambert Locks and on down to Quebec City. Unless you have that poetic something within you crying out to be on the Atlantic, chances are you'll turn back at Montreal, which is a pity. Past Montreal, the river is no longer Canadian; it belongs to the world. Once the river stops being channelled and shunted and girded by locks and canals, it blossoms into a mighty panorama. Once pleasure steamers operated along the river between Montreal and ports like Tadoussac, Baie Comeau, and Sept-Îles. The last year Canada Steamship Lines ran the service, I was on holiday in Quebec with the children and, on the spur of the moment, decided the river trip was something not to be missed. I was right. I stood at the ship's rail and caught the fever. Since then there's been something inexplicably romantic about being closer to the sea than to the inland Lakes.

By the time the waterway reaches Quebec City, the effects of the ocean are dramatic: the fresh-water tides are fourteen to sixteen feet high, and the currents suddenly reverse themselves as the tide changes. At night, we'd anchor *Serenity* close to the shore to stay clear of the shipping lanes while allowing sufficient room for the boat to swing on the tide without drifting aground.

The trip through Quebec had been magnificent; there had been more than enough wind in the right direction to sail below the historic Plains of Abraham and the Château Frontenac. Our sightseeing cruise took us through a gaggle of local yachts in the middle of a regatta, before we returned upstream and berthed at the Quebec City Yacht Club.

East of Quebec City, the terrain becomes quite mountainous; Mont Ste-Anne loomed large and beckoned to the skier in me. We were now starting to see fall colours, and sheets of slate-grey clouds scudded overhead, sliced occasionally by a shaft of sunlight.

Piloting the river was challenging and, because there was always some routine maintenance to be done – a loose cleat, a fouled line, a broken steering vane, or blocked plumbing – we were a busy crew. By late evening on September 1 we anchored wearily at Cap Chat, having spent the day mostly under power and continually at the wheel, while ogling the beauties of the Mt. Joli range.

From the time we tasted salt, the river had begun to sprawl outwards. I had very detailed, large-scale charts (it takes more than one hundred to map the whole St. Lawrence), so our only problems were caused by my piloting errors. Because *Serenity* drew only five and a half feet, it was often possible to take shortcuts across the serpentine routes designated for larger vessels. Even at low tide, I could count on four or five feet to spare taking the shortest distance between two points. It required a weather eye for barren knuckles of rock, little islets that are often barely submerged at high tide. These treacherous rocks are indicated on the charts, but I called the shots wrong a few times. Once we passed within six inches of crunching on one of them. The needle of my echo sounder leaped as if taking cover, and I was just able to put the wheel hard over to avoid foundering.

The Gulf was a preview of the sea to come. From time to time we saw dolphins. The morning we left Cap Chat, we were followed for an hour by a number of them, arcing gracefully under the water and into the air. If we clapped, yelled, and stamped our feet they would come close to the boat and put on a show in apparent response to our applause. One grey morning, as we moved slowly through a fleet of fishing boats, the dolphins suddenly exploded all around us; other times they merely surfaced at a distance and took no notice of us.

As we were rounding the top of the Gaspé Peninsula and about to swing south into the Gaspé Channel, we spotted the spout of a whale about a half mile away. He leaped into the air to a height almost equal to his sixty-foot length, landing with a crack on his side and an opening bloom of spray. Spellbound as we were, we were glad he had kept his distance.

A few hours later, I saw another whale spout about three hundred yards dead ahead. Concerned about attracting his attention by any sudden move, I held my course and we passed about five yards off each other's port – in accordance with the rules of the road. He was an immense beast, grey and covered with black crustaceans. As his head passed the cockpit the great blow hole emitted a noisy blast of foul-smelling breath.

The names of the tiny villages down along the New Brunswick coast are heavy with the history and religion of the early Breton settlers: Ste-Marthe-de-Gaspé, Ste-Anne-des-Monts, Gros Morne, Mont Louis, Petit Vallée. What sea captains pushed their clumsy, square-rigged ships upriver, tacking back and forth, day after day, against strong and unchartered currents, to open up the interior of a new land?

Cloridorme, Rivière au Renard, Cap des Rosières, Cap Gaspé – the coastal settlements ticked by as we moved southward in variable winds and gloomy dampness. At 3:30 p.m. on September 3 we sighted Percé Rock, looking just like it was on a postcard.

From time to time we'd find isolated pockets of anglophones, bracketed by French-speaking villages. The temperature became noticeably warmer as we went south, not so much because of latitude but because of warmer currents that swirl around in the Gulf of St. Lawrence. Each night we would anchor offshore one of these tiny coastal villages. John would row in and invariably strike up some acquaintance with the locals. This came in handy when we needed diesel fuel. The fishermen were only too happy to oblige, although selling "purple gas" – coloured, government-subsidized fuel for fishing vessels – was illegal. My French is virtually non-existent, so I had to rely on John's halting efforts and smooth charm; neither failed us.

The people along this coast had no interest in our destination, whether Halifax or the Caribbean, but were quite talkative about our port of origin. The sophisticated Québécois or Maritimer may loathe Toronto, but The Big City is a fascinating topic for these rural folk, who rarely leave their own province.

Our usual very early start proved to be a mistake along the New Brunswick coast. All of the little lobster and inshore fishing boats are up and about at 4:30 a.m. and waste no time getting out to their Gulf fishing grounds – without running lights.

The mist is heavy on the water, and all you can hear is the swelling and fading *thug-thug* of engines, as forty or fifty boats race in different directions in the pitch dark. I had lights all over *Serenity* and thought it unlikely *they* would hit *me*; I feared for them. But somehow, each fisherman senses where the other boats are, even the odd private yacht foolish enough to venture into his territory.

The lobstermen "run a range," dropping a line of lobster pots marked by flag buoys. Each range, a mile or more long and three hundred yards from its fellow, is demarked by some all-but-invisible system involving shore landmarks. By the time the sun burned off the mist, we found ourselves threading *Serenity* through an orchard of little flags of different colours, neat as the pattern on an Acadian quilt. Each of these boats, often little more than a few planks holding up a huge diesel engine, is skippered by a dour and accomplished free-enterpriser, who goes about his business with a practised eye, an economy of motion, and an unshakable faith in the sea.

Our only stop on Prince Edward Island was at Borden, on September 6, where we pumped out the holding tank and took on fresh water. By the end of the day, with good southwest winds, we made it through the Northumberland Strait to Mulgrave, Nova Scotia, on the Strait of Canso, which separates Cape Breton from the mainland. We were just ahead of a southerly gale and in the hurry to find an anchorage, I managed to foul the anchor-rod in the propeller. I've made a lot of sailing mistakes in my time; but never had I wrapped a five-eighth-inch nylon line around a propeller, and I don't know why I chose that particular moment to do it.

John and I took turns for most of the night down in the icy water with a waterproof flashlight trying to free the line. In the end, for fifty dollars, I hired a local diver who returned to the surface, proudly holding two shaggy rope ends. He'd cut it. I could have used a knife for free the previous evening! I found the Cape Breton wharf cowboys very friendly, and our plight provided some distraction for the locals, all of whom had smart solutions – none of which involved going into the water themselves.

The next morning, at dawn, I was up like a kid at Christmas. The wind that had howled east the night before was now in the northwest, perfect for sailing through the Strait. We'd been in salt water for a week, but now we were on the brink of hitting the real ocean, a vast expanse of water on which we could set an easterly course and sail for weeks without touching land.

We had the wind on the port quarter as we came out of the Strait of Canso at about eight and a half knots; we were met by the sentinels of the Atlantic: rolling monster waves, which *Serenity* took like a terrier, her bow biting cleanly into them and throwing back a fantail of icy spray. We were both in foul-weather gear and harnesses, ready for the ocean's best punch. I was almost giddy with apprehension and delight; I had never experienced sailing like this. We even forgot to look astern, until we'd lost sight of the Canso light.

I was searching for the first of a series of white buoys that delineate a "highway" to Halifax, which follows Nova Scotia's south shore about twenty miles out. We'd have to stay up till dawn watching for the lights, but stopping for the night would involve threading our way into one of the obscure inshore harbours in dangerous wind and sea. Besides, the boat was sailing beautifully.

I was told later that the swells were close to forty feet high – I'd estimated twenty – leftovers from a gale that had been buffeting the coast for a week. *Serenity* roared down through the trough of each wave and almost drifted up to the crest of the next. A couple of times during the night, the wind dropped, and everything that could move had to be lashed down very, very tightly while we were under power. The engine was a puny force against the gigantic waves, and the wishbone boom had to be tied amidship to keep it from whipping back and forth across the cockpit with each wave cycle. Still, it was a clear, moonlit night, a night that banishes troubles and sets the mind to dreaming and invites you to count the stars. . . .

William Zeckendorf.

There is no question that Denver, Montreal, and, to a lesser degree, Los Angeles would not be the cities they are today if it had not been for the vision of William Zeckendorf.

There were other pioneers of the 1950s and 1960s, imaginative builders who conceived, designed, owned, and managed major office buildings and shopping centres. I was privileged to learn my trade under some of these men and to become one of "Zeckendorf's boys."

Another of those boys, in 1958, was James Soden, a partner in the prestigious Montreal legal firm of Phillips & Vineberg. Soden had been sequestered to act as secretary of Webb & Knapp (Canada) Limited – the Canadian arm of Zeckendorf's empire, incorporated primarily to develop Place Ville Marie. The original estimate for this project, a couple of years earlier, had been $55 million, later revised up to $75 million. I had been involved with Webb & Knapp's enterprises elsewhere in the country and had only been called to Montreal on a few occasions when Zeckendorf was in town or there was some major issue that required my presence. Although Soden and I were to work closely together over the next two decades we really knew very little of each other at this particular time. Receiving a request from him, therefore, to come to Montreal on an urgent matter was not particularly surprising since most matters were "urgent" in those days.

On arriving at our offices in the Dominion Square building I was ushered to Soden's office, stacked with unsigned contracts, bound documents, law books, and all of the other paraphernalia of a lawyer cum businessman. Soden, a few years older than I, was clearly agitated as he announced that he had just been appointed financial vice-president of the company. As an assistant vice-president myself, a full vice-presidency was the next jewel in the crown – so why was he so upset? Apparently, in digging through the files he had come across a revised estimate of the cost of Place Ville Marie that far exceeded the budget of $75 million accepted by both our board and the public. In my capacity as the construction expert of the team I was being asked to go to New York with Soden and break this news to Zeckendorf.

We both knew there was no possible way we could lay our hands on conventional funds to make up the difference. Although Metropolitan of New York was the likely source of a $50 million first mortgage there was no secondary financing or equity in sight to satisfy the new requirements. Having just joined the company I had to dig hard and fast to come up with an explanation as to why a $75 million cost estimate could have soared out of sight in less than two years. I found out. It was not my job to lay the blame but rather to solve the problem.

At that time the Lockheed Electra turbo-prop was flying from Montreal to New York. This particular aircraft had developed a nasty habit of falling out of the sky at disquieting intervals and, prior to its eventual withdrawal from service at the request of the FAA, it was being used on short runs around the country. I used to do everything possible to avoid flying the Electra, but Electra it was on our flight to Idlewild. We had talked ourselves out on the plane, rehearsing and bracing ourselves for the conflagration we knew was ahead. Now, as we drove through Queens towards the Manhattan skyline, we were as silent as the vast cemeteries flanking the highway. Both of us would have sold our souls to delay the encounter.

The elevator at the Madison Avenue office of Webb & Knapp carried us to the top floor with undue haste. In the ill-defined, but tastefully decorated, reception area we waited for the Master's call. Off to the right was a wide window overlooking a roof garden with a bronze statue of a muscular, well-endowed female. Straight ahead was the now famous, round Zeckendorf office. Singled out from other architectural elements, it was an island on the sea of beige carpet that covered the vast empty floor, a twenty-foot diameter cylinder running from floor to ceiling. A clerestory of glass at the top allowed us to see the lights inside. Legend said that they would glow blue if he was buying and red if he was selling. At the moment, they were white.

The summons came. We entered the great round office and the Great Man actually looked small as he rose from his desk and asked us if we would have coffee. We came to the point.

"Mr. Zeckendorf – sir, we have been working on the estimates produced by I.M. Pei, the architects, over the past eighteen months. You will recall that the cost of PVM was originally to have been $55 million and you know that there have been increases, because of design changes, to $75 million." Here Soden took over. "Our most optimistic calculations show that the cost will now be in the range of $105 million . . ."

Soden was stopped dead by the look on the man's face. Zeckendorf was staring at a point somewhere in the heavens. And smiling.

Zeckendorf reached for his intercom. "Bill, get in here!"

He leaned back, drumming his fingers on the arms of his chair.

"Billy," as we called him, arrived in a matter of seconds. He greeted us with his characteristic clipped phrases.

"Bill, listen to what the boys just told me."

Soden repeated the news.

"Bill, we've done it!"

Young Bill looked as incredulous as we. Zeckendorf shifted; both hands were now behind his head and the smile broadened. "Jesus Christ, Bill, don't you understand? We are now building the most expensive building ever created by man!"

On the way down in the plane Soden and I had nervously joked about the possibility that, in the ways of mythology, we, the messengers of defeat, would be executed. Instead, we were feted, wined, and dined in Zeckendorf's penthouse dining room – white-coated stewards and fluttering maids hovering about the ebullient host and his two thoroughly relieved but confused guests.

Back in Montreal, in order to give reality to the story, we had to raise the money. We did so by diverting funds destined for other projects in Canada to PVM, issuing a unique debt instrument known as a "self-bailing debenture," and above all, sweet-talking our suppliers into postponing their requests for payment. To this end we created a rather woolly agreement known as "suppliers' equity." This was simply a euphemism for "we can't pay you now, so how would you like to wait." Otis Elevator, Canadian Pittsburgh Industries, Comstock Corporation, and dozens of other sub-trades flocked, albeit sometimes reluctantly, to accept "suppliers' equity" in return for lucrative contracts and the prestige of being associated with what was now the world's most exclusive building construction project.

All of this was a valuable addition to my education.

When it came to starting Yorkdale – another multimillion-dollar project, the largest enclosed shopping centre in the world, I hadn't enough money in the bank to meet one week's payroll. The Bank of Nova Scotia was prepared to advance us funds but only if we could come up with a construction mortgage that would be an effective guarantee.

I discovered the Chase Manhattan Bank. Where the Canadian chartered banks feared to tread the Chase Manhattan was more than happy to venture. In their New York office I found that every decision-making executive was an Irishman, and I searched back deep into my own ancestry to find a specious common bond. Once established, however, the Chase was a joy to do business with compared to our hide-bound local institutions.

Before having arranged my financing, however, I had let a general contract to Taylor-Woodrow whose head office was in England. After construction had been underway for about three months Mr. Frank Taylor, the managing director, flew over from London to meet this young man in Toronto who, according to his local office, was forever postponing payment of his justly due accounts.

We met over dinner at the Westbury Hotel and I, with great conviction, told him of my success with the Chase Manhattan of New York, and it was just a matter of time before the first cash advance would be forthcoming. Taylor listened with substantially less enthusiasm, but did agree to give me thirty days before he took action. In the meantime construction work was to be cut down to a minimum and no further obligations incurred on the part of Taylor-Woodrow. I was prepared to pledge my home, car, wife, and children to secure those thirty days. I worked like a man possessed to conclude my deal with the Chase. Our lawyers, Blake Cassels & Graydon, under the energetic leadership of Chris Miller, negotiated and drafted day and night to complete the documents necessary for the complex mortgage agreement.

We made it. Chase Manhattan signed, I signed, the Bank of Nova Scotia signed, and work resumed on the Yorkdale site. Frank Taylor and I remained friends for many years.

Zeckendorf eventually had to seek a financial partner – the Eagle Star Insurance Company of London, England. Because of Webb & Knapp's inability to meet its financial obligations to the English, the control and ownership of Place Ville Marie, Yorkdale, and two other shopping centres under construction eventually fell into other hands. The man who had had the vision to conceive the Mile High Plaza in Denver, UN Plaza in New York, and the world's most expensive building, Place Ville Marie, was now merely a spectator – removed from the scene by the same vision, imagination, and energy that had placed him at the top of his industry a few years before. Even in bankruptcy Zeckendorf continued to make history. Until his dying day he directed the unwinding of his empire under the incredulous eye of the receiver.

Winning was important – but *trying* to win was really what set my juices flowing!

Just after dawn, there was enough wind for us to sail into Halifax harbour, off to starboard. I phoned ahead and we were met at dockside by a friend, Mike Novac, who took John and me out on the town. We spent a couple of days sightseeing before flying back to Toronto. I saw *Serenity* securely berthed and told the club I'd be back in five weeks.

On that night run from Canso to Halifax I realized that *Serenity* could take it, and that I was a good enough sailor to handle the wind and very high seas. It was as though I'd passed a test of confidence: right or wrong, I felt sure I could handle, single-handed, open-ocean sailing. How long I could stay on the ocean was yet to be determined; but I would make the next leg of the journey. At the very least I would go to Bermuda. Then I could decide whether to cross the Atlantic to the U.K., strike into the Caribbean, or take the southerly route, the start of the circumnavigation that was just forming in my mind.

I don't think I said more than ten words to poor John on the flight back to Toronto. I was making mental notes: I would need more charts for Bermuda, the South Atlantic, and the Caribbean islands; I wanted to make minor modifications to the boat; I needed to extend my insurance to cover a longer trip. The business matters that I had to attend to I heartily resented, and the five weeks, so full of preparations and activity, seemed to crawl by.

CHAPTER FIVE

I *CLEARED MY SLIP AT THE ROYAL NOVA SCOTIA YACHT*
SQUADRON EARLY IN THE MORNING, OCTOBER 21, 1979.
Behind me the club was almost deserted except for the fuel
dock attendant, who filled my tanks for the journey to Bermuda and opined that I was mad.

"A couple of boats tried it a week or so ago. Just heard
they're sitting in Hamilton harbour, with all their sails blown,
one with a broken spar, the other with half of its rigging carried away and the deck sprung open." The numerals ticked
over on the pump. "Wrong time of year. Storms come one
right after the other!"

Besides the pessimistic dock man, no one but Wanda and
Joan Hammell knew I was leaving. I had flown out of Toronto
a couple of days before with no more farewell than a perfunc-
tory "have a good trip" from the Air Canada ticket agent. In
Halifax, I remained vague about my voyage. It is hard to
understand why I was so secretive, but at the time it was part
of my sense of what it meant to go "solo." Part of my
reticence may well have been a subconscious fear of failure. If
I lost, the defeat would be my secret: no one would know –
and tell – that I had tried and failed.

The fog was lying thick on the water when I cleared the fuel
dock. Working off the harbour chart, I eased *Serenity* under
power from sheltered waters into the open Atlantic. Every fifteen minutes or so I had to cut the engine to listen for the bell
buoys in the harbour entrance and to check their locations on
my chart. Visibility never got better than a quarter of a mile. It
was 0900 hours when I cleared the rocky outline of Chebucto
Head. I cut the engine, raised my sail, and by noon I was ten
miles south in open sea.

On L/C-4003, "Cape Breton to Cape Cod," I had pencilled a

line from Halifax to the bottom of the chart, indicating a true course of 184° or 205° magnetic. With a decent wind, I should reach Bermuda in about one week.

Charts have always held a peculiar fascination for me. The particular chart I refer to was one of hundreds I had onboard. They allowed me to plot my positions using my sextant and Loran C, to determine the depth of water beneath me, and to identify shipping lanes. They allowed me to measure, with great accuracy, my distance from, and the configuration of, any coastline.

Especially valuable was the *Pilot Chart*, on which I relied for my October departure despite the fuel dock attendant's warning. The idea for a monthly pilot chart came from Matthew Fontaine Maury, the American pioneer in oceanography. It divides the sea into 5° squares and lists the percentage of calm and gales, and the wind velocity and direction in each block for each month of every year. This information is based on many thousands of observations made for specific months during a period of more than one hundred and twenty-five years. A wind rose in each 5° square indicates the prevailing direction and strength of the wind. Current direction and strength, storm tracks, limits of ice, fog, magnetic variation, atmospheric temperature and pressure, water and air temperature, reported icebergs, and more are all predicted for the month. All this data – updated monthly – is shown on one chart, a masterpiece of the cartographer's art.

I also carried *Coast Pilots*, *Sailing Directions*, *World Index*, and the ever reliable British Admiralty publication, *Ocean Passages of the World*. I also had tide tables and a directory for worldwide marine weather broadcast, which I could pick up on my shortwave radio. I was leaving the safety of the North American shore with more data, aids, and instructions than most commercial vessels carry.

In five-foot swells, *Serenity* was doggedly clawing her way out into the Lahave Basin fishing area against a force three wind (seven to ten knots). My stomach was the one part of me that never liked sailing. For years I had popped Gravol if there was any sign that I was going to be moving through any seas. It is essential to take the pill *before* you enter rough conditions: there is no defence once the sickness has struck. I took my first Atlantic Ocean Gravol in the Strait of Canso a month earlier. John and I took one every four hours during our night run to Halifax. Now, alone, I was ready for my second pill since leaving port. The plan was to take this treatment for the first couple of days and then to hope that constant exposure to the sea would immunize me from *mal de mer*. It worked: I never was seasick during the whole voyage.

By the time the sound of the last fog horn had faded in the mist behind me, I had the self-steering gear operating, the sail set, a cup of hot coffee in hand, and nothing to do. I was on the great Atlantic Ocean, and I was alone: I had joined Slocum, Gerbault, Chichester, Graham, and, of course, Sir Alec Rose, with whom I'd corresponded shortly before my departure. I carried Sir Alec's letter of good wishes as a talisman.

I was afraid, with the fear of a child anticipating a ride at the fair ground; a delicious apprehension tempered by a blind trust in the manufacturer of the roller coaster. I trusted *Serenity*; I trusted my knowledge and experience; I trusted my sextant and my charts; I trusted my own body and in my own perception of a God.

I didn't feel I had any special dibs on God any more than I believed that God was on the side of the Cincinnati Reds because the batter crossed himself. I confessed to no priest; I acknowledged no church, but I believed that, unless I made a complete ass of myself, there was a Higher Power who would provide all my needs. Not all my wants. It's up to me to earn my "wants." The supermarket provides groceries; if I want to have them I must pay.

I stripped off my foul-weather gear and retired to the warmth of the cabin. I lay on my bunk revelling in the sound of the passing water and Tchaikovsky's Fourth Symphony on the tape deck. The wind had risen to force five (seventeen to twenty-one knots), and my speed was about five and a half knots: I could make Bermuda in less than seven days. My rhumb line or desired course was 4° west of true south; but I was heading slightly east because of the southwest wind. By late afternoon, I was out of radio contact with the shore; my last weather forecast had told me to expect "clearing, a rise of winds to twenty-five knots and seas of some ten feet." The anticipation was exhilarating. All my senses were in tune with the sea, the wind, and the fog. Now I was *really* a sailor – a single-handed sailor – and I was on my way.

Dinner consisted of yogurt with granola and two glasses of milk. The weather report had been accurate; with seas like these I wouldn't be getting many hot meals without more practice on my gimballed stove.

I went on deck to check my course and the weather. My masthead tri-colour light and anchor light were not working; I had only hull-level running lights. I was going to pass through fishing areas, and the danger of being run down by one of the huge fishing trawlers that prowl east of Georges Bank was very real. With poor visibility, a fully loaded trawler could pass through *Serenity* without even feeling a bump, so I hoisted a portable battery strobe on a halyard, well up the mast.

By the second morning at sea I had put away ten hours of sleep, albeit fitful, with one ear cocked for trouble, and had to go on deck only once during the night. My first night alone at sea! I was now making four to five knots under a single reef, approximately one hundred and ten miles south of Halifax. I got one Loran fix the previous night and another in the morning, which showed that I had just crossed over the Continental Shelf and was now more than 6,000 feet above the ocean floor. I was also twenty or thirty miles east of my desired course because of the wind direction. This was to continue, forcing me to buck hard into the wind on a starboard tack.

Shortly after noon, I heard the first of many sharp, rolling *booms* off to the west. It was an aircraft breaking the sound barrier, permissible over the ocean but rarely heard on land.

My evening Loran C fix indicated that I would leave the fishing areas during the night to enter the main shipping lanes between the U.S. East Coast and Europe; I would cross the tracks of the transatlantic freighters for the next two or three days. I'm not sure these behmoths would even notice my little catboat, but I was eagerly watching for them; the first I saw was merely a smudge on the dusk horizon. Although I never knowingly came near a collision, it is quite possible that I experienced a close scrape or two while asleep; I'll never know for certain.

When I woke on October 23, I was sweating in my bunk;

bright sun was lancing through the ports. The air was warm and humid and I trailed my hand over the side. The water temperature was about 60°F. I knew I had entered the Gulf Stream – and right on schedule. In one day I had gone from a ski jacket to a bathing suit, and I took my morning coffee sprawled in the cockpit, revelling in sunshine on my white, unweathered skin. I opened up the cabin as much as I could, hoping to air out the last traces of the all-pervasive fog that had followed me since Halifax. The previous day I had noticed water standing in beads on the bulkheads above the bunks, and the cabin sole and the galley counter were covered with a damp, salty film.

The sunny interval was glorious, but brief; during the next twelve hours the weather deteriorated. By late afternoon, I was back in wool and oilskins; the clouds had lumbered in and the temperature had dropped. Before I turned in I took a cautionary two reefs in case the wind came up overnight. With the double tuck I was showing less than 200 of the boat's 540 square feet of sail. And a good move it was.

During the early morning hours, I was wakened to the sounds of vibrating rigging and thrashing canvas. The wind had risen to a full gale. At 0420 hours I eased myself through the partially opened companionway. My spray-soaked spotlight could barely pick out the sail, which appeared to be half torn off the mast. I couldn't hold myself on deck, much less determine the problem and make repairs in the angry and violent motion. Reading about similar conditions I had been certain that I could respond knowledgeably in the situation; when the gale struck I was not an experienced ocean seaman. I felt violated and helpless. There was nothing I could do but set my impotence and fear aside and sleep – tied to my bunk.

Dawn, OCTOBER 24:
0740 HOURS:
Last night the wind rose to a full gale. This is my first experience and I found it more exhilarating than terrifying even though the boat is in danger and I have lost a good part of my rigging. Mountainous seas are crossing my path, the sail is torn half off the mast, and I cannot make any repairs in this weather. I am down below, where almost everything has been

thrown out of its proper place: my clothes are wet, and there is water all over the cabin sole; books, magazines are all mixed up with the sea water and food.

At the moment there is nothing I can do except stay below and let the ship be tossed about, listening to the sail flog itself off the mast. It's just become light enough to see the size of the waves, and they are absolutely beyond belief. I can't make coffee, because if I stand up I get thrown about the cabin. If I injure myself I really will be in serious trouble, so I am going to stay put and hope that things settle down sometime during the day. The log showed us surfing with the waves at up to 12 knots.

0900 HOURS:
I have just come down from the deck, where I tried to get the boat on some kind of course, but it is impossible. The track has been separated from the mast. How I am going to sail from here on in, is something I don't know or at the moment care about. The boat seems to be handling the waves reasonably well, although I am taking an awful lot of solid water right across the deck and down into the cockpit. The companionway must remain closed, and I am down below as though I was in a submarine, with the boat tossing about showing green water at the portholes almost constantly. The sail, which is impossible to set, is flogging and vibrating the whole boat.

0910 HOURS:
I'm lying down below, listening to music; there is nothing more I can do. The sun is trying to appear. It seems rather obscene that the sun should come out at this particular time with all the carnage and violence around me. Last night the sun set in a red sky, and I thought of the old adage: "a red sky at night is a sailor's delight." But I guess this disproves that.

1010 HOURS:
I have just come down from the cockpit. I was attempting to haul in the mainsheet so as to cut the

59

*flogging down somewhat and discovered there were
only about five or six sail runners left and most of
the sail track has been ripped from the mast. The sail
came away from the mast entirely and was left flying
like a huge balloon or spinnaker off on the leeward
side.*

*I was able to haul it in by turning on the engine
and heading the boat up into the waves. I'm now
lying-a-hull, and it is relatively quiet with no sails
flogging and the boat rising up and down on the
swells. My situation is relatively safe. I am being
driven north and east at probably 6 to 7 knots and
will undoubtedly lose at least a day's run. How I am
going to sail from here into Bermuda, I have no idea.*
1230 HOURS:
*I have been lying-a-hull for a few hours now and the
wind is howling outside like a pack of angry animals.
Inside the motion is getting quite violent. If the
waves should crest, which they are starting to do,
and I get caught in one of those crests, I could be
capsized. I'll give it another fifteen or twenty
minutes; then I think I might put the stern towards
the waves by dragging some lines behind me, so the
sea will pass under me rather than pitching me over
sideways.*
1300 HOURS:
*As expected, one of the big grey beards crested on me
and turned me on my beam end, so that everything
across the cabin came rolling at me and I got hit on
the head with the radio directional finder.*
*Fortunately there is very little blood, and I now have
almost anything that can move down on the cabin
floor. The wave also sent a solid body of water
roaring across the cabin and into the cockpit, and the
boat seemed to stand up to it reasonably well. Unless
things get worse, I think I'll ride it out just as I am.*
1520 HOURS:
*Still lying-a-hull, broadside to the wind and the
waves. The wind has increased substantially in the
last few minutes; it is singing in what little rigging I*

*have, and laying the boat over on a heel by just
pushing on its mast. Looking out the portholes there
is nothing but white out there, I can hardly see the
water.*

1800 HOURS:

*The sky is blue, and the clouds are fluffy, and the
sun is going down. However, the sea is just as angry
and the wind just as strong, and all of this is
beginning to get to me. I'll have to lie-a-hull again
tonight, and the motion of the boat will be
sickening. If I do get off tomorrow it will be with a
mainsail just barely fastened to the mast. How I am
going to sail at night from here on in I do not know.
I'll try to put the small tri-sail into operation, which
I haven't been able to use yet. Now appears to be the
proper time.*

*About every ten minutes a particularly large wave
will crest under the starboard – which is the weather
side of the boat – and will lift it up and send
everything crashing across the cabin. I'm used to it
now, however. Since I haven't been turned over, it
would appear as though I'm going to be able to last
this one out.*

For the rest of that day, and all through the next, I could only
lie-a-hull and wait out the storm. Much has been written
about laying-a-hull. It involves dropping the sails and letting
the boat find its natural position as it drifts downwind under
the force of waves and gale. Alec Rose wrote: "It is safer to lay-
a-hull. That is to strip off all sails and let the yacht go with the
sea and take up her own position . . . although the boat is
often thrown about unmercifully . . . she would lie-a-hull in
the very fiercest of storms." Never having performed this
manoeuvre before I had to rely on the advice of others and, as
it turned out, this advice served me well. What I lacked in
comfort I gained in security, as time and time again *Serenity*
withstood the battering of sea and wind as if born to the task.

Despite my fascination with the storm and the frantic work
arising from it, I suffered spasms of gut-wrenching fear. A particularly savage wave would trigger a surge of adrenalin, or

Serenity would suddenly feel like a slipper being shaken by a puppy – with me in it. Mostly, however, I succumbed to a terror of uncertainty. Would I capsize? Was there too much water in the cockpit to stay afloat? When the mast broke, would it drive a hole through the hull? Would I be injured? If so, would I ever reach shore? Time was the great tranquilizer: by the second day I was taking it all in stride, sleeping occasionally and listening to my music. The gale began to wane and swing to the south.

My position was equidistant from Halifax, New York, and Bermuda. The wind direction said New York, logic said Halifax; but I insisted on Bermuda. For a while I was at a loss as to my exact position because of the clouds; and inexplicably my Loran C worked only after dark. So it was 2015 hours before I got a fix and found that the storm had blown me close to 200 miles east of my course. I raised the small tri-sail, which moved us at an agonizingly slow three knots on the long upwind beat. There was no way I could batter those waves and that wind without the engine.

The combination of power and the life-saving tri-sail was working well. Before altering my course to the southwest I checked *Serenity* from stem to stern for damage. I found only slight dislocations in the electrical system and a broken hose in the engine room. I was back in business!

Quite unrelated to the storm, however, a cassette was jammed in my tape deck. I had more than a hundred tapes onboard, from Chicago jazz to opera and a careful selection of the classics. I was going to miss the music. I enjoyed my own company, but music had always provided a tranquil companionship that bordered on addiction.

Having found how far off course I was and that it might take me another four or five days at least to reach Bermuda, the vastness of the ocean became very real. Before, it was only something about which one reads in books, but now I could see how plotting errors of only a few degrees made Bermuda into a mere speck on the chart. I hoped my Loran fixes would become more reliable. They didn't.

The aloneness of all this started to get to me. I kept thinking there was someone else onboard, an odd, unsettling feeling I couldn't shake. I would swivel around half expecting to see

62

things that I knew weren't there. I so expected someone to talk to me that I wound up talking to myself. Worse, a fragment of a children's rhyme rattled endlessly, maddeningly in my head: "Half swan, half goose, Alexander was a swoose. . . .

A few weeks earlier I had decided that the Bermuda run would be my first ocean passage. I needed a shakedown cruise. I had not been tested physically or psychologically for the rigours and solitude of single-handed sailing on the open ocean. Nor had *Serenity* been put through her ocean trials, even though she had proven her abilities on Lake Ontario. A straight run from Halifax to Bermuda would be about 740 nautical miles. It would take about one week and at no time would I be so far from land that I could not reach shore under diesel power.

Now here I was, six days out of Halifax, and because of the gale, a long four days to Bermuda, with seventy-two hours' fuel in the tanks: I'd need at least one full day under sail alone if I was going to make it. Fortunately the wind rose from the northeast and by mid-afternoon it was blowing up for another full gale. I had jury-rigged the small tri-sail on the mast with loops of nylon cord, after hacksawing away the bent and useless track. It seemed to relish the force eight wind, as long as it was abaft the beam. The boat needed no auxiliary power, handled well, and was making good speed. I had no interior lights on the starboard side; it was probably a short caused by salt corrosion. The salt and damp had penetrated virtually everywhere.

By late afternoon the wind was gusting to force nine and, after dropping the sail, I could accomplish little. I lay down, listening to Bermuda radio, which I was able to pick up on the AM band. I was closing in on my target. George, my self-steering mechanism, was keeping us on course and seemed to dampen the boisterous careening leaps *Serenity* made, prodded by the following gale. My Nonsuch was excelling itself; at six knots under a bare pole I had every chance of actually shortening my projected voyage by a day and a half. It was a welcome prospect, because I was longing for a hot shower and a dry bed: I was loath to use my precious fresh water, even though I had a seventy-gallon capacity, as I was not certain how long it would be before I made a landfall. My bedding never did dry from soaking during the gale a few days earlier.

Whenever I went to the cockpit to check course and rigging, the wind and spray burned my skin. If I faced aft and opened my mouth slightly, the wind would swoop in and puff out my cheeks like a chipmunk's. It was so strong that it lifted the eyelids off my eyeballs.

The helpless mainsail was in the lazy-jacks, but part of it was catching the wind and dragging down under the water. Hanging from my safety harness, drenched with spray and solid water, I took more than two hours to lash it securely against wind and waves.

By late morning on October 28, the sea had calmed considerably, and I used the lull to air out the cabin and clean up. During the storm, my normally fastidious nature could only go into suspended animation as books and papers accumulated in soggy piles and everything that could shift position did. I opened all the portholes, the companionway, and all my hanging lockers. There hadn't been a dry spot anywhere, but now everything was drying beautifully. I even took time to shave off a four-day growth of beard before going on deck to cut the mainsail off the lazy-jacks, manhandling and stowing 540 square feet of heavy wet Dacron below, and still leaving elbow room for the skipper.

Moments of high drama – storms, danger, and problems – tend to dominate tales of the sea. My routine following storms was reasonably disciplined and predictable. I tended to sleep eleven hours a night, half-waking at unusual sounds or to peer at the hand compass I kept beside me to make sure the self-steering gear had me on course. I'd plant in my brain the course that I wanted, and if it didn't read that when I half-woke, I'd go topside and adjust George accordingly. I suppose I got eight hours real sleep over the eleven hours.

I'd wake about four or five a.m. and would go to bed at sundown (five or six p.m.), except on calm nights, when the beauty of the night sky sometimes kept me up until the wee hours. On those nights, only four hours' sleep was enough, and I slept like a baby in all but the stormiest conditions. I absorbed like a sedative the distinct but pleasant smell of surface weeds that are the hallmark of the Gulf Stream. The babbling of the water heard in the cabin was a natural surrogate for my silenced Mahler, Verdi, and Beethoven. I was truly happy.

The couple of days sailing I'd managed by the morning of October 29 left me with ample fuel to reach harbour, even if I had to power all the way. Of all the equipment on board, the two-cylinder Volvo engine had given me the least trouble. I had assumed, after being knocked down several times, the engine would have crank-case oil up in its cylinders or, at the very least, there would be oil in the bilges. In fact, the only oil that got into the bilges was from some halibut liver capsules I spilled. *Serenity* smelled like a Newfoundland fishing dory until I was able to flush it out, but the engine performed beautifully.

Eight days out, about breakfast time on October 29, I acquired a passenger – not the phantom companion that had spooked me a few days earlier. It was a small land bird, rather like a starling but with a better tailor – a lot of green and yellow specks. I called him Irving, for no particular reason. From the way he moved in, sat on my shoulder, noshed on soggy Ritz crackers (and anything else that wasn't nailed down), and stood lookout at the masthead, it was clear he was hitching a ride to Bermuda. Indeed, he stayed with me almost all the way. We spent a lot of time together in the cockpit because, whenever we were under power, I had to be at the wheel. George got a rest in more-or-less becalmed conditions, while Irving perched by the hour on the hub of the wheel, staring intently at my navel, and crapping constantly.

I was nearing Bermuda. In only hours I would learn whether my navigation could locate a speck of an island in the middle of the Atlantic. After years of working with the sextant, and teaching it, I was putting myself to the proof: and it would be a simple pass or fail! My Loran C navigation was questionable; however, I had developed great faith in my sextant. Theoretically, my calculations should locate me within five miles of my actual position on the chart. I could then steer a course for Bermuda that would avoid the dangerous coral reefs guarding its northern approaches.

In fact, I knew that, as long as my position was more than fifteen miles north of the island, a sextant error would not be too serious because I could use one or two quite unnautical methods described by friends back at the Port Credit Club. Their first tip had been simply to watch for commercial aircraft landing. It's obvious they are not dropping down into the sea; they must be hitting a landing strip on an island, and in my position, that island had to be Bermuda. The other system involved the use of a cheap radio I had bought in Halifax. This small receiver had a built-in aerial that picked up a Bermudian AM station. If I rotated the radio until the volume was at its lowest point, the radio would be pointing directly at the station's antenna. I could steer that course and, theoretically, arrive within sight of the radio tower. As a purist, however, I felt that both tricks were cheating; I really wanted to do it the way it had been done for the past four hundred years.

> OCTOBER 30:
> 0730 HOURS:
> This should be my last day out in the open ocean. I'm 90 miles from Bermuda, and it looks like another day of powering, which should get me to within 25 to 30 miles of the island, certainly close enough to make radio contact.
> I didn't sleep too well last night. I had to get up about 1230 hours and adjust the sail and the wind vane because a squall came through. Unfortunately, it didn't last; and I made very little distance.
> I noticed, in doing my calculations last night, that I had made a minor plotting error in my course yesterday, which took me about 15 miles farther west than I wished to go. It has lengthened my trip by only about 7 miles, but it was annoying.
> The sun has not come up yet and I look around me and see this huge sea. There really have been no surprises on this trip; I think it was just the sheer power of the gales, the winds and the waves that impressed me. You must see them firsthand to understand the uncontrollable fury of the ocean. It can never really be described in books or seen properly in movies.
> Every backup system onboard has been used. At

the moment, I'm powering, instead of sailing; I'm using extra fuel from the jerry cans; I have used my sextant when it appeared my Loran was failing; the sail up is my storm tri-sail; my masthead running light gave out for a while and I had to use my hull lights; one wind vane broke in a gale and I had to use a replacement. Just about the only thing that I've not had to use is my life raft, which is still heavily lashed down on the main deck and, I hope, will not have to be put into play before I arrive in Hamilton. The only system I did not have a duplicate for was my music, and I've been without Beethoven, Tchaikovsky, Mozart, and Brahms for the past four or five days. This has been a serious deprivation.

0800 HOURS:

Irving just turned up; he's a late riser. I've already been up 2 hours. He must have spent the night under the dinghy on deck. I'm not going to feed him today. Maybe that will keep his bowels from being as active as they were yesterday. Food goes in, is processed, and shoots out his birdy rectum, all in sixty seconds. The deck and cockpit are awash with seawater and bird shit.

0935 HOURS:

Only 71 miles to go; but I've just been checking the charts of Bermuda and approaches, and it appears there is no safe way to get in there after dark. I'll probably try to get as close as I can and then either lay offshore or anchor in "Five Fathom Hole," which is recommended by the Bermuda sailing instructions. This anchorage doesn't look very protected on the charts, but I'll be contacting Hamilton Harbour radio for advice before I make up my mind anyway.

1020 HOURS:

I just tried to raise Bermuda radio on the VHF without success. In case they heard me I told them I was all right and I would try again in about two hours.

1100 HOURS:

I cut the engine and started to sail. I've got a good

wind off the port quarter, and I'm doing only about 4 knots. If I continue at this speed the rest of the day, I'll avoid getting too close to the island before dark. I'll be able to sail during the night and arrive at the approaches the first thing in the morning. I think of all the options this would be the most prudent.

1500 HOURS:

I just got a Loran fix, the first I've been able to get in daylight for quite some time, confirming my noon sextant sight, and I find I'm making about 12° westerly leeway. Even though I didn't trust the Loran, I'm correcting east; an error to the west could put me into the coral. I've got about 50 miles to go according to this latest fix; at a fairly slow speed, I should be arriving at the approaches at about first light tomorrow morning.

Irving is making an absolute pest of himself. I'm not feeding him today and it's driving him bonkers. He's crawling all over me looking for food, biting my elbows, earlobes, and so on; but I'm not weakening, and he'll have to wait until we get to the island before he gets food.

1830 HOURS:

I'm still about 30 miles away from the point where I should be seeing St. David's Light and 34 miles from seeing the Gibb's Hill Beacon. If I don't see them, I'll have to ease up a bit. I'm edging eastward to make certain I don't run on to the coral reefs. There is also a strong east wind blowing about force 5, which is moving me along at a pretty fair clip. I do not want to find myself having to work off a leeshore if I am in too close.

1915 HOURS:

Seven hours to go before I could possibly spot the closer of the two lights but this is the "moment of truth." I keep going out on deck looking at the horizon where I expect to see it. If I don't see it, I've made a mistake; if I see it too soon, I've also made a mistake and I've got to start to make some adjustments. The only correct thing is for it to

appear right on time, plus or minus a half an hour.
This is the real goal of the whole trip: being able to
find a little island in the middle of the Atlantic
Ocean.

OCTOBER 31:
0330 HOURS:
I've just had four hours' sleep and was awakened by
my alarm about the time I should be able to pick up
Gibb's Hill Beacon or St. David's Light. I got up,
looked out the companionway and, sure enough,
there they were, right off starboard bow. I've still got
to pick up a buoy to make absolute certain where I
am; but at least I found my island. However, I've got
a lot of coral to pick around tonight. Once that's
over with, I'll hit dry land, a fresh water shower, and
a good hot breakfast.
0655 HOURS:
I've now taken sight lines on all the known lights on
shore and I'm now fully familiar with my
approaches. I've also run in close enough to pass over
the coral shelf with shallow water showing on my
echo sounder. I'm now just running in and out until
there is sufficient light to see where I'm going. I've
taken a hot shower and shaved. I feel great! The sky
to the east is getting light. One more pass and I
should be able to enter the narrows and inner
harbour.

Although the lighthouses and beacons make sailing much easier, Bermuda still has a reputation for being treacherous. Mark Twain wrote that "Bermuda is like Paradise, but one has to go through Purgatory to get there." He was doubtless referring to the menacing and widespread reefs that the Spaniards marked on their charts as *ya de Demonios* (the Island of Devils). The whole group is the only visible evidence of an extinct volcano, and the reefs are the most northerly in the world.

So I was swinging in from the northeast, to reach the east end of the islands via the narrows that would take me into St.

George's Harbour. To the west and north there were three buoys with flashing white lights, each spaced about two and a half miles apart, to warn of the reefs.

The approach was euphoric! With only my sextant, tables, quartz watch, and book-learning, I had navigated the North Atlantic. I had found Bermuda. Only then did I realize how much it meant to me to "do it alone."

I entered the cut at 0730 hours. There were the red-and-white buoys to port and black buoys to starboard – my first exposure to the International Buoyage System. "You are in line with the channel when you can see a narrow beam light on the westernmost tower on the cut's north side," claimed the Bermuda sailing instructions. I had no idea what it meant, and I didn't care!

After a week and a half of high seas, and a wind that had only last evening dropped below thirty knots, it was almost unsettling to be on a mirror pond in the lee of mountains. When I nosed into the Market Wharf under power, I had come 905 miles in ten days, one hour, and seven minutes.

I had seen the last of Irving some time earlier. As we sighted Bermuda, he had begun to be a pest. I cuffed him away and he went into a sulk. I knew he was still on the boat, and suspected he was huddled under the life raft. Sure enough, half a mile out, he emerged, only to be caught by the force six wind that blew him overboard. He flew frantically to reach the stern, just missed, and fell into the water. I even contemplated turning *Serenity* around in a predictably vain attempt to rescue him when he fluttered out of the water, apparently spotted St. David's Light, and lit out for land.

By 1000 hours I had cleared customs. The very smartly uniformed, personable young man in Bermuda shorts who handled my paperwork seemed only mildly interested in my port of origin, my journey, or my arrival, but was very helpful in suggesting where I could moor. For the time being I was rafted alongside a boat from Rhode Island and was secretly pleased to find that in suffering through the same storms, it had sustained far more serious damage than *Serenity* had. Misery doesn't necessarily love company, but a shared misery can sometimes be reassuring. There was one fifty-foot ketch moored nearby with seven young people aboard. They had been cruising down the coast from Cape Cod to Georgia when their boat was caught in my two gales, and they were blown 300 miles out to sea. Bermuda was their nearest landfall, and they had reluctantly limped into port.

My feeling of well-being had a slight edge, however. I had come through the adventure with no physical or emotional scars, but *Serenity* had let me down. The track torn from the mast and the minor breakdowns that had plagued me over the past ten days had me questioning my confidence in her. Could she withstand any more abuse, which was sure to be inflicted upon her if I ventured out again?

I searched out Meyer's Marina at the west end of St. George's Town and arranged to have *Serenity* cradled out on their travel lift and have the bottom gone over. They were to repair some minor damage to the aft end of the keel. New tracks were to be bolted on to the mast. They could repair the boat and I'd pick it up in March – before then the weather would be too uncertain to venture further. I was thinking that I might quit, and sell the boat. It was perfect for sailing those waters, and I'd probably get a good price for it. But I never sought a buyer and made no decision during the week I spent relaxing and sightseeing.

I'm an inveterate tourist, especially when I'm alone. I looked in at St. Peter's Church in old St. George's, one of the earliest Anglo-Saxon communities overseas from Britain. The church was its first gathering place and site of its first Parliament, in 1620. In the churchyard are some of the oldest crypts and headstones I've ever seen, grim evidence of harsh times and early death.

The rest of my time was spent wandering in St. George's or Hamilton, Bermuda's "big city," and sampling the local food. After my self-sufficiency during the trip, I was glad to have others wait on me; and, while I detest preparing food for myself, I didn't shy away from new and exotic fare, well served in fine restaurants: from Pawpaw Montespan and Hoppin' John, the former a meat-and-fruit treat, the latter a local variation on baked beans, to pan-fried fish and a local version of Key Lime Pie.

It was in Toronto, after a brief flurry of arrangements for the repair and shipment of new parts, and reactivating my business, that I felt really low. The Hinterhoeller boatyard couldn't have been more helpful in arranging the shipment of new tracks that would be securely bolted to the mast. Still, for a week or so, I felt ambivalent.

I don't recall how or when I regained my confidence and enthusiasm; perhaps it was my overriding compulsion to finish what I started. Moreover, I realized that I had reason to be proud. By anyone's standards, the Halifax-to-Bermuda run is tough. I'd come through two brutal North Atlantic gales, navigated successfully, and raised that tiny island. I'd arrived healthy and happy. What was I bitching about? *Serenity* had not let me down; we had just begun to test ourselves. There were a million experiences out on that ocean – maybe a whole world to girdle.

But in the global scheme of things Bermuda is only an island off New York.

It wasn't long before I was ferreting through the catalogues at the chart shops and making plans for the next leg. I bought charts and sailing directions for virtually every eventuality: a direct crossing to England; a crossing to Capetown; to Lisbon – even being carried off course, down the South American coast. I had become an unrepentant chart addict. I was itching to get back to my boat and out to sea again.

CHAPTER SIX

M EYER'S YARD IN ST. GEORGE'S, BERMUDA, IS A PLEASANTLY RAMSHACKLE PLACE, CLUTTERED with all manner of boats and paraphernalia: cradles, lumber, chains, cranes, cable, and canvas, all overlaid with the unmistakable smells of resin, marine gel-coat, okum, wet tarps, and sawdust. There is always some activity, but little of the sense of urgency that I felt and might have hoped for when I arrived there late on the evening of March 3.

As the customs agents explored my luggage, they found a lot of things tourists don't carry: charts, a quartz clock, stainless steel shackles and hardware, and other bits of marine gear. They were very polite, but very slow. All my "suspicious" belongings were left in bond, to be reclaimed later with a sworn affidavit from the Meyer's foreman saying he was installing it on a Canadian-registered vessel.

By the time the punctilious officials were through, there wasn't a cab left at the airport stand, and it was pouring rain. Only a piercing whistle – the kind that has won me many a cab over the competition in Toronto, London, or New York – was able to catch the attention of a taxi straggling past on a nearby road.

By the time I was deposited at Meyer's, it was past ten p.m. I was damp and out of sorts. I wandered aimlessly about the yard trying to pick out *Serenity* from among the dozens of ghostly winter-stored yachts. It was raining mercilessly and the dark was punctuated every few seconds by the rotating beacon on the U.S. Naval Air Base across the bay. During one burst of light I caught sight of *Serenity*'s plumb bow and topsides beaded with water and streaked with black coral grime.

I found a ladder and, collecting my luggage, which I had shoved under the protection of a nearby hull, I climbed up and into *Serenity*'s cockpit once again. In the intermittent flashing of the airport beacon I saw her decks were coated with rain-soaked dust, which grated underfoot. I unlocked the companionway, went below, and turned on the lights. Everything was as it had been when I left her four months before. I was home. The propane flame on the stove brought relief from the rain outside. I brewed some coffee, stowed my gear, and slipped into my bunk for a dreamless sleep.

By nature, I am impatient; and, although this trip was intended to break a lot of my old patterns, I still wasted no time in letting the foreman know I was steamed up that none of the work I had ordered had been completed – most not even started! I'd phoned a few days earlier and knew that *Serenity* wasn't likely to be in the water by the time I arrived, even though the new track and the stainless steel bolts had arrived weeks ago. The shipyard was to redrill the holes in the mast, tap the threads, and bolt the track on – a long and tedious task, done with the mast out of the boat, lying horizontal on work horses.

The lad assigned to the job was certainly willing, the more so with me first peering over his shoulder and then working with him. It was only three days before the mast was stepped and we had the boat back in the water, but it seemed to be forever.

Besides the new, stronger track, there had been other, fiddley bits to be done: some fibreglass repair, painting and trim work, and installation of the marine equipment I'd imported. I went over the track installation as scrupulously as an astronaut examining his air supply line.

In my restless prowling about the yard, I became friendly with an innovative young man named Tom Lemm from Baltimore, who was earning his keep doing odd jobs for the boatyard. Lemm was working his way around the world on the schooner *Le Papillon*, which he had built himself. Over the occasional drink, sometimes at the White Horse Tavern, sometimes lounging on *Le Papillon*'s deck, he gave me good advice that sailing books can't impart, particularly about how to sail around the Caribbean. He assumed, as I did at the time, that my destination would be England via the Azores – a reasonably popular route – and that I was going to do some island-hopping first.

"If you're going to poke about the Caribbean," he told me, "don't take the obvious way, approaching from the west. Sneak up on it from one of those eastern islands, like Antigua, and circle back. You'll put in to a lot of ports that way, and get the benefit of the Gulf Stream and the prevailing winds. You'll wind up at Fort Lauderdale, Palm Beach, or thereabouts and be in a perfect position to swing across to the Azores neat as you please."

"What about the weather?" I asked.

"Starts to improve about May."

But this was March! I couldn't wait two months, despite Tom's warnings and the admonitions of three or four people in St. George's who had made the same trip. Between warnings, I got a lot of information about weather, currents, Caribbean coral reefs and harbours, and two recipes for flying fish.

Because of the damage that I had suffered in the North Atlantic gales of the previous fall I still had some doubts about *Serenity*'s ability to withstand another battering. During the winter I had decided that the most prudent move was to take another "shakedown" cruise, this time from Bermuda to the Caribbean. From there I still had numerous choices! I could head east to the Cape Verde Islands, then north to the Canaries, Gibraltar, Portugal, or England. I could work my way northwest to the U.S. East Coast, and from there to the Azores and Europe. There was also island hopping in the Caribbean or – the ultimate challenge – from the Cape Verdes across the equator into the great Southern Ocean and on to Capetown, the first leg of a circumnavigation.

My plan had been to make for Cockburn Town, San Salvador; but Tom Lemm and other sources of Caribbean lore and legend convinced me that I should head for the Leeward Islands in the Lesser Antilles, putting into Antigua or Guadeloupe.

By midday, March 6, the new track was mounted, the mast stepped, and *Serenity* launched. Had I waited a couple of more days I could have seen to some minor items, but I knew that I could handle them just as well at sea. Once again I went over every inch of her hull, rigging, and systems, assuring myself that we were ready for anything the Atlantic might hand us.

Tom Lemm gave me a list of U.S. radio stations and their frequencies for offshore and high-sea weather broadcasts, and the poet in him sent me off with the hand-written benediction:

May Poseidon grant safe passage and stay Boreas' hand.
May Austers breath upon your sails waft you to distant land.
When Apollo smiles and Bacchus pours, take Aphrodite by the
   hand
Enjoy, enjoy and think of me on some secluded strand.

I rounded the spit buoy at about 1330 hours and the island was out of sight within the hour. I had checked out with Bermudian customs and retrieved my flare pistol, which I had had to turn over to the officials on my arrival a few months before. A courteous young customs man wished me a bon voyage with the admonition that "nobody leaves Bermuda at this time of year – terrible storms all the way south!" Shades of my departure from Halifax. The March *Pilot Chart*, however, predicted that the 840-nautical-mile run to Antigua would be blessed with variable winds, few of which would exceed force four; air temperatures between 68 and 75°F; light ocean currents with a westerly set; moderate seas; and a sea surface temperature of about 75°F. I chose to believe my pilot chart – and I was right.

We were on a course of 145°, close-hauled and a little east of my rhumb line; but the westerly set of the Gulf Stream would compensate for this. At six knots, I was having a magnificent sail under clear, sunny skies. The wind was beginning to shift to south-southwest and the seas were a bit choppy. My Gravol was working; it would be a few days before I could wean myself from it. *Serenity* and I were back where we belonged, on the open sea bound for exotic shores. All the strains and cares of living with the Earth People dropped away. Tom Lemm's Boreas, god of the wind, was doing just fine.

Before my trip I had heard and read a lot about piracy. Yachting magazines are full of horror stories and self-defence tips. Such piracy has none of the romance of Robert Louis Stevenson. Today's pirates have a neat and cold-bloodedly efficient way of going about their business: after masquerading as a disabled fishing vessel, or using some other subterfuge, they simply knock the crew over the head and dump them

76

overboard to drown. No trace – the perfect crime. I did not carry a gun. To have one implied the intention to use it – and I had no will to shoot. Once onboard they were the experts: brigandage was their business, not mine. But one's only real defence was to avoid them, and I went to great lengths to do so. No lights at night, no casual discussions ashore, and I radioed a false course report as I left the harbour, about 45° from one I was on. I'll never know whether these extraordinary precautions were effective or necessary.

On my first night out I slept well, as I almost always do when the boat is underway, although the sails needed attention a couple of times during the night. I was up at dawn, scrubbing the remains of the boatyard off my deck and cabin sole. I shaved, made breakfast, and idly puttered about while the coffee brewed, then took a steaming mug on deck to revel in the subtropical weather. The wind had dropped to about two or three knots and my southerly progress slowed accordingly; but it was immensely soothing to sprawl on the cockpit cushion with one leg hooked up on the lee side, naked as a jaybird, sipping a cup of coffee and soaking in the hot sun. I was in no hurry.

We were married in Ottawa on May 20, 1950. Everyone said we made a wonderful-looking couple at the wedding. I had fallen quite uncontrollably in love with this girl two years earlier; twenty-one months ago I had, much to my own surprise, asked her to marry me. (I was working as an architectural draftsman in Toronto and thought I would be more than content to lead a marauding, hedonistic bachelor life forever.)

Although we had met and dated a few times Wanda really dropped into my life when she and her parents came down from Ottawa to Clayton, New York, where I was sailing our boat *Canuck* in the LYRA regatta. My brother and I had bought *Canuck* for $750. We replaced almost every plank in her hull, spliced her mast, and installed complete new rigging and sails to the limit of our budget. She was a lovely twenty-five footer, and we raced her well.

As the evening sky glowed red, Wanda and I would wander by the shore of the St. Lawrence and talk together within the sound, but not the sight, of the alcoholic revelries of my fellow yachtsmen. We talked about all those things that must be gently touched before one can fall in love. She was engaged, but this did not deter me for a minute: I was determined to marry this girl.

I announced my nuptial intentions to my unwashed and foul-mouthed crew members on the return trip from Clayton to Toronto. The verbal abuse laid on by my friends aboard *Canuck* should have sunk the boat. At nineteen years old, life is a carnival; girls are for taking, not for marrying. I had injured my hand during the regatta and I received a leave of absence from my employer. I hitchhiked to Ottawa and proposed; she accepted.

It was very important to me that my mother approve, and she did. She warned me, however, that I should be careful how I told my father, as he quite correctly felt I was too young to assume the responsibility of a wife and family. (In 1948, of course, marriage arrangements did not include a second income: Wanda would not go out to work.) We need not have worried: my father was almost as happy as I was.

I had a beautiful fiancée, the approval of my parents, and shortly thereafter a site on which I would build her house – not ours, hers. Designing and building this house was to be almost a sacrament: I was in love and I intended to be a model provider.

During the twenty-one months of our engagement most of my earnings, which had been going to support the family, went into building the bridal cottage and buying a ring. By our wedding day, the ring was paid for and the house financed. After a frugal but joyous honeymoon through New England via Quebec City, Mr. and Mrs. David Philpott embraced the joys of married life on Toronto Island. There may have been happier grooms, but I wouldn't have believed it.

At the end of the first year Wanda presented me with a son. Her labour began on a foggy evening in early April, and by two a.m. we were dramatically speeding across Toronto bay in the cockpit of the Harbour Police patrol boat, spray in our faces from the pounding bow waves, my arm around Wanda – the very image of the strong male protecting his mate in danger. I leaped from the police boat to the dock and straight to the waiting cab. Jumping in the back seat, I barked, "St. Michael's

Hospital," to the driver and closed the door. It wasn't until we had pulled out that I realized my very pregnant wife was still making her way up the slippery ramp of the Harbour Patrol wharf. She was in labour fifteen hours. I visited the small labour room as often as the nurse permitted; but these were the days before "joint-venture" births were popular, and I, as the husband, was considered something of a nuisance.

At 5:15 p.m. on April 3, 1951, Dr. Gerry Solmes emerged from those unknown inner rooms of the hospital and showed me my eight-and-a-half-pound son: his eyes were closed, his face wrinkled, and his head pointed; he looked sticky and wet all over, but he was mine and I felt like God!

After a second fifteen-hour labour, at 5:15 on another April afternoon three years later, Wanda gave me Wendy. God and I did it again!

By 1960 I had a large home, two cars, and a swimming pool. The visible stamp of success. But during the fifties, social conventions demanded certain rituals of the upwardly mobile suburban junior executive. One of these was joining a church and sending our children to Sunday school. Although both Wanda and I had had fundamentalist Protestant upbringings, neither of us was drawn to the suburban church by religious fervour. I had, however, a mild curiosity. What was this all about? It had to be more than just a sanctimonous country club. It was not a compulsion to conform, but rather a lack of interest in non-conforming, that carried us to the church with its Christian and non-Christian activities intertwined and unidentifiable.

For reasons still not clear to me, I adopted as one of my many avocations the study of the Bible and church history. Within a couple of years I was superintendent of the Sunday school, on the Session, a representative of our congregation to Presbytery and later to the General Council of Canada. Typically, I could not enter an organization – or company – without eventually taking charge.

During this period I was wooed by Al Forrest, later the editor of the United Church *Observer*, to study for the ministry at Emmanuel College. I agonized over this decision for almost a year. The "show biz" appealed to me. As a lay preacher I belched wisdom from the pulpit and received unctuous praise from the newly converted. I loved the studying, the history, the tradition. I loved the idea, but I really didn't like people that much.

Counselling troubled souls, holding the hands of the dying, and manoeuvring through the politics of the women's association all repelled me. In a fit of petulant cowardice, I turned the decision over to Wanda: if she could cut the mustard as a minister's wife, then I would enter Emmanuel College (I had already been accepted) for my Bachelor of Divinity. When I think back on it now, shifting the responsibility to Wanda was the cruel act of a frightened man caught up in an agony of conscience. My faith went far enough that I knew rejecting this opportunity was a slap in God's face. And I didn't want to be the slapper.

I didn't go into the ministry. Instead we took up skiing. After all, it's a matter of what the suburban family of an upwardly mobile junior executive does on Sunday. One can choose church, television, winter sports. We opted for skiing. I resigned all my offices in the church and we joined a group of forty or fifty families who had rented some property in the Caledon Hills about forty miles north of Toronto. Here again, without any particular desire on my part, I became a founding member and director of the Caledon Ski Club.

I threw myself into this club with the same enthusiasm I had applied to the church. Wanda and the children loved it; we skied every Saturday and Sunday, sometimes racing home so Stephen could be on the ice in time for one of his weekend hockey games.

Inevitably I also became involved in this. I became manager of a hockey team, guiding my ever-losing but happy tribe through four years of competition. I was a rotten hockey player, although I loved the sport, so I could only impart those sporting and competitive instincts to the boys that I felt would both win games and give them a solid grounding for manhood. How successful I was in the character-building phase I will never know, but I certainly was a twenty-four-carat flop in the "winning" department. Although every lad turned out to each game with the skills and attitudes that I had instilled in him, we failed to win more than one or two games each season.

It was a happy time, ideal years. We were a textbook example of rigid conformity and success – the classic nuclear family.

After my father lost his money during the war years, ambitious and energetic as he was, he never really accepted his diminished situation. I provided substantial support for my parents and sisters before I got married, and my mother would always consult me on practical family problems during the following ten years. Wanda was party to these problem-solving sessions and eventually she took over my mother's role completely. In April, 1960, we learned that my mother had terminal cancer. My mother and I had always been extremely close. Ours had never been a warm, demonstrative affection but rather a strong empathy and understanding based on tacit Anglo-Saxon love.

We watched her die over seven months. She had been a strong, beautiful woman with an unshakable faith in God and in the goodness of the human spirit. As she lay in her hospital bed shrinking to a spectre of sickly yellow skin stretched over a skeleton, something died inside me as well. I remember trying to tell her that I had been made an assistant vice-president with Webb & Knapp (Canada) Limited. She had always expected me to achieve, now I could tell her that the world had recognized my success and I had a title to prove it. She never heard me. I sobbed uncontrollably at her funeral.

After my mother's death Wanda arranged the engagement parties, weddings (I had the funerals), pre-baby showers, post-baby showers, christenings, and the endless organizing that fall to the head of the clan. Although I felt strongly that my brothers and sisters took advantage of her from time to time, she appeared to enjoy both the responsibility and the strong family bond that had been lacking in her early adult life.

We were happy. We knew we were happy because we had everything that happy people had. We did everything that happy people did. We said all the things that happy people said; we may even have thought all the things that happy people think. The mid-sixties brought clouds of restlessness that I could taste but not identify. I did nothing about it because, of course, I was happy.

After almost fifteen years on shore, I bought *Wanwind* in 1966. She was a beautiful thirty-two-foot sloop. I loved it but it was a millstone around the neck of my family. The children unwillingly learned to sail; and when Wanda insisted that the children "go out sailing with Daddy," they did their duty with frozen smiles and sullen eyes. Wanda was wonderful; but, sandwiched between a man who had bought a boat ostensibly so the family could enjoy the summer together and two children struggling against the confines of the suburban family corral, she could hold out only so long. I ended up sailing the boat alone, a harbinger of a life to come.

Eventually I sold *Wanwind*, not because I was forced to but because I wanted to: she had intruded in our lives like an unwanted guest.

The storm clouds loomed a little higher and darker on the horizon, but we knew we were happy. And we were happy because we were in love; it was unthinkable that we should not be.

I had some difficulty when the wind dropped. The sail slatted petulantly above the rolling deck and the oily swells. When the topping lift parted at sundown one night, I dropped the sail into the lazy-jacks until I could effect a repair in the morning. The wind came up at dawn but my idle sail had been chafing against the deck all night and I had to waste two hours of excellent sailing time repairing the resulting hole.

Later, one of the hooks on my new radar reflector halyard broke and the reflector fouled in the leach of the sail. I had also left the Loran on and had to endure the roar of my engine while recharging the batteries.

A boat is very much like an active child who can't help getting skinned knees, muddy shoes, and a bloody nose. You have to roll with it, and I certainly did; but I couldn't help wishing for a good gale to put some ginger into the trip!

After three days at sea, I'd only covered 267 miles of the now 950 miles to Antigua. About 100 miles had been added to the distance because of adverse winds and current. The capricious winds were a continuing annoyance as I was required to adjust George, my self-steering gear, every few hours at the whim of the weather.

By late on March 9, however, the wind had picked up to about force five from the southwest, and I was right on course doing about five and a half knots. That night was a dome of stars. There was no moon, but some planets were so bright they were reflected in the sea. The next day was idyllic; I even found a flying fish on board – shades of Hemingway and Ernest Gann. I cooked it with one of my Bermudian recipes, but found it very tough and full of tiny bones.

As usual my Loran C wasn't working and I was getting simultaneous readings about sixty miles apart. So I resumed taking sextant sights. The failure of the electronic navigating machine and the success of my own skills smugly pleased me. My confidence far exceeded my navigational abilities; but, after all, I had zeroed in on Bermuda, and I could certainly find the islands of the Caribbean.

My tape deck had been repaired in Bermuda and I spent my time below reading and listening to music. There is a smooth thrill when the cabin is filled with Schubert, Chopin or Mozart while you're reading the adventures, and following in the wake, of Chichester, Slocum, or Naomi James. I had little real work to do and stayed as close-hauled as I could to the southerly wind. I was travelling in a southeasterly direction, to the east of the proper track for Antigua, but I had been told that this was the best way to pick up the northeast trades. After all, the trade winds were what cruising was all about.

By dawn on the fourteenth, the wind, which had been increasing steadily through the night, was approximately force six (22-27 knots). *Serenity* asked for no relief and I carried a full head of sail on a broad reach hitting as high as nine knots from time to time. I was now in the tropics, crossing the Tropic of Cancer at 0650 hours with a nod of recognition.

Five days earlier I thought it might take weeks to tack into Antigua; now I was beginning to count the hours till my arrival. *Serenity* was handling beautifully, and I certainly had all the ginger I could ask for.

Within a few hours, the wind was working up to force seven, strong and steady – a perfect sailing blow. I reefed. Taking in one tuck, I eased the pressure on *Serenity*; she responded by surfing on the crest of the waves at speeds in excess of twelve knots. This was the most invigorating sail I'd had since leaving Halifax, and my speed was, by far, the fastest I'd ever experienced. This was March the 14th. At about 1030 hours the wind began to drop and I shook out the reef, putting *Serenity* under full sail again and holding a speed between seven and a half and eight knots. A beautiful sail, superb conditions, and right on course for Antigua.

At 1055 hours the mast broke.

With barely a sound, and taunting in its slowness, the sail, wishbone, and rigging toppled into the sea over the starboard bow. *Serenity* wallowed lifeless in the six-foot swells. Leaping against the pull of my safety harness, I tried vainly to save some of the gear now hanging just below the surface of the water. It was hopeless. The jagged butt end of the broken mast drove into the hull like a battering ram every time *Serenity* sunk into a trough.

In minutes I had cut the lines that held the tangled mess to the boat; it drifted down and out of sight. I was left with a four-foot stump of a mast, one small sail down below, some ingenuity, and 370 miles to go. I'd attempted to see whether or not the wishbone could be salvaged as a jury rig – possibly standing it on end against the stump of the mast and guying it with some of the lines. However, it was fastened securely to the mast, which could not be moved, and I had to give up before serious damage was done to the hull.

I was dumbfounded! There had been no indication of a problem, no warning. After my initial shock, my strongest emotion was disappointment rather than concern; I was going to miss sailing the trade winds.

An hour later I was sitting at the wheel with the engine throbbing monotonously. The deck was splattered with blood from a deep gash I'd received in my left hand while cutting away the wreckage. Both hands were rope-burned and bruised. In logging the incident later I discovered that the whole tangled, heart-breaking mess was on its way down to the Nares Abyssal Plain, the deepest spot on the Atlantic floor, 19,200 feet below.

Survival is a strong disciplinarian, and I got to work. The wind had swung round to the west, so the self-steering vane did a reasonable job of keeping the boat on course under power; I was able to go below and make some fuel calculations. According to my figuring, I had left Meyer's with thirty-five gallons of fuel. Three gallons had been used to charge my batteries. At ten miles to the gallon, my Volvo would take me to within fifty miles of my destination – and then quit. My only comfort was that it would get me into well-travelled shipping lanes where I might attract rescue or assistance.

About noon on March 15 I saw my first ship since the accident. A large freighter was passing about a mile off to my stern. My VHF radio was useless as my masthead aerial was at the bottom of the sea, and I had neglected to hook up my auxiliary antenna. I could let go a smoke flare and he probably would have stopped and given me a can of diesel fuel. But, for some inexplicable reason, it became very important to me to make a landfall without any help.

Even if I had too little fuel, I could rig my stormsail somehow. Sooner or later, I reasoned, by sailing down wind, I would hit one of the Leeward Islands. That night I ran under power, cajoling George into keeping us on course every few hours. A wind-activated steering vane is not intended to operate under power. It was only because I had a fairly strong breeze on the beam that it worked at all – and then only moderately well.

Although offending my nautical pride, I had to admit that it did a far better job than I could have done manually – I tried and couldn't keep within 15° of my desired course. My accuracy and attention had gradually deteriorated during the previous night, dulled by fatigue, boredom, and a crushed ego.

I had been humbled before, but never by the elements. All the previous battering to my ego had been in the cross-currents and storms of business.

In the autumn of 1977, New York City was about to default on its debt interest. Corporations were fleeing to the Sun Belt, and the city's reputation for law and order had never been worse. This particular day had been hot and, for me, tiresome. I had spent it with Paul and Albert Reichmann, prowling up and down Sixth Avenue and along the East River near Wall Street looking at fifty- to seventy-storey buildings. All were empty and in deep financial trouble. Edward Minskoff, a Manhattan broker, had been trying to convince the Reichmanns to buy a package of eight buildings once owned by the Uris Building Corporation and now being dumped by National Kinney for $350 million.

My company had enjoyed a happy and mutually profitable

relationship with the Reichmanns since 1973, when I had assisted their expansion into Alberta, British Columbia, and Quebec. Now they were looking at potential acquisitions in New York; Minskoff's enthusiasm was matched only by my cynicism.

Paul had made his position quite clear: "New York just won't close down." Albert was slightly less positive, asking how soon (not "if") the city would be able to solve its problems. They felt the land beneath the buildings was worth more than $350 million, but I believed that acreage value was only a function of what it could produce in income, and I could not see any potential for adequate income within five years.

Two weeks after our return to Toronto, the Reichmanns bought the Kinney properties for $25 million less than Uris had received for them. They had also picked up three buildings from Penn Central. Olympia & York now owned more than 12 million square feet of New York office space; it could produce, at best, only seven to thirteen dollars rent per square foot. Two years later, rents had risen enough that New York's second largest landlords were now showing a profit. By 1981 the income had quadrupled to more than $2 million per day.

I was among the many who recommended strongly against the purchase.

An earlier humbling experience took place in Montreal September 13, 1962, on the much publicized opening day of Place Ville Marie. It was first-rate Zeckendorf: a prestigious office development built over the "hole" – the ugly web of tracks that ran a few hundred feet below street level from Central Station under Dorchester almost up to St. Catherine Street.

For four years my heart, soul, and every waking hour had been dedicated to Webb & Knapp projects, and I would have given my right arm rather than miss the ceremonies. Full of youthful self-importance, and a shiny new title of "vice-president," I was certain that the whole universe was waiting for Place Ville Marie to offer itself to a grateful world.

I was standing at the southeast corner of Mansfield and Dorchester waiting for the light. In a moment I was to cross over and, I felt certain, become part of history. Also waiting for the light were two English-speaking suburban matrons chattering away. Suddenly, one of the women pointed across the road, and said excitedly, "Oh look, someone has filled in the hole!"

I stood in shock and disbelief. The pinnacle of my life's work had been reduced to filling in a hole. My thirty-five-year-old ego was shattered.

These two assaults on my pride, spaced fifteen years apart, had made it clear that, although my ego still needed massaging, it had become sufficiently bruised and scarred that I could now concede that the centre of the universe lay somewhere other than right behind my belly button.

The noisy *thwugga-thwugga* of the diesel and the ugly motion of the boat without the stabilizing sails kept me just under the surface of sleep all night long. Without the load of the mast, the boat tended to bang down, slapping on the waves, and I woke feeling like I'd been physically beaten.

There was a brief rain squall and I rushed to indulge in the luxury of a fresh-water shower; but the squall perversely passed on before I had rinsed off. I had to go below and use some of my precious fresh water supply, but I must admit I felt like a new man.

> *MARCH 16:*
> *0915 HOURS:*
> *At 0830 hours this morning I emptied two five-gallon jerry cans into the tank – and that's it. According to my calculation I will run out of fuel about 60 miles from the nearest island. I've been making plans for all kinds of Rube Goldberg rigs that will allow me to run with the wind, but so far none will stand up. This is my project for the day: I must come up with something that will allow me to move the boat in a westerly direction without using the engine before I run out of fuel.*
> *1335 HOURS:*
> *I feel that to jury-rig now would be best, rather than wait for improved weather conditions. I have spent the morning rigging up the storm tri-sail on a mast made of a mop handle, a broom handle, two oars,*

*and a boat hook – all well lashed and guyed to the
stump because such a flimsy mast is not going to
stay up on its own but will need stays of some sort.
To fly the sail as low as possible I raised it with the
luff-side parallel to the deck so that the foot is
excessively long. As soon as the wind caught the sail
the boat hook bent over, but it held, and with a few
adjustments to the "shrouds" it is still holding and
I'm moving along at between 2 and 3 knots. If this
rig holds out for just one whole day, I will have
picked up my 60 miles and can make port under
power.*

In fact, the rig did remain intact; and I made St. John's harbour in Antigua.

I checked and double-checked my navigation several times a day, taking as many as six sextant sights and averaging the readings to try to achieve maximum accuracy. On the evening of March 17 I set my alarm clock for 0600 hours, my estimate of when I would be within five or six miles of the island of Barbuda, just north of Antigua, my first landfall.

My confidence in my navigating abilities were rudely shaken when I awoke in the morning of March 18 to find myself a mere half mile off Barbuda. I was parallelling the low sandy coast, in calm water, at about two knots. (I had shut the engine off during the night and had travelled under sail alone.) There was little danger, although I was close enough to see people walking on the shore and to hear dogs barking; but on a slightly different bearing, I could well have grounded.

I fired up the engine and changed course to 215° to cover the twenty-five miles to Antigua. I seemed to have every conceivable chart of the Caribbean onboard, except one of St. John's harbour. However, St. John's, at the north end of the island, seemed a likely destination, if only because it would be the first anchorage I'd sight.

Fortunately, I was able to follow a large cruise liner in, so I knew which channel to take. There appeared to be no specific yacht mooring; in fact, I found it peculiar that there were no pleasure craft at all in the rather grubby harbour. Finally I found an available mooring spot against a commercial pier, next to a tugboat. As I was docking, the propeller dropped off: *Serenity* was truly helpless.

Knowing I'd have to clear customs, I hopped ashore and trudged up to a likely looking prefab shed. I was quite a sight: sunburned, with bleached hair, wearing a rumpled RCYC T-shirt and a pair of cutoffs that had seen better days. There was an ugly bruise on one thigh, a big bandage on my left hand, and my fingernails were filthy.

The customs shed was largely taken up by a long counter, behind which stood a stalky, uniformed officer. He saw me come in, but did not acknowledge me and continued to chat with a woman at the counter. After I stood for what must have been twenty minutes, shifting from one bare foot to the other, listening to them gossip, I said, simply, "Excuse me."

Deliberately not looking my way, Mr. Customs said, more loudly than was necessary, "Wait until I'm finished."

It was ten minutes more before he slowly turned in my direction, looked me up and down, and said, "Come back when you're properly dressed."

I didn't want to ruffle his feathers, but I didn't know what the hell his problem was and said so.

"I don't speak to people in bare feet," he said icily, and turned his back.

I stomped back to the boat and angrily put on my shoes, came back, and told him tersely where I was moored and what had happened. He couldn't have been less interested. He simply put my passport and papers in a drawer.

"How long are you going to keep those?" I asked.

"I've got to check things out," he said enigmatically, beckoning me towards a little cage in the corner, a wooden frame covered with fence mesh, with a small wooden bench inside. He shut the door, slapped a padlock on the hasp, turned heel, and disappeared.

From my cell I could see the empty customs hall, which was a large shed with a view of the harbour. Opposite the window was the counter. Chairs of every conceivable design lined the walls. No one entered the room. The counter remained unattended and the chairs empty. I could hear sounds of casual activity around me but I never saw a soul for more than eight hours.

What was happening? No passport, no telephone, no protection from the law – I was scared! Not since the North Atlantic gale had I known fear, and this was even more frightening – here there were no rules or defence. I could disappear forever into the militaristic swamp of this Mickey Mouse republic. Drowning at sea would have, at least, been heroic – this was totally without class. Anticipating the worst, my imagination took off on a morbid frolic that only ended with the sudden appearance of Mr. Customs, who slowly removed the padlock and opened the door.

Without any explanation I was handed my passport and ship's papers as he ushered me out. I told him I needed a tow to a permanent mooring and his only reply, as he slammed the door, was "See me tomorrow."

I went back to *Serenity*, very dispirited and feeling helpless.

The next morning, I waited for hours to see him again only to have him dress me down for being moored illegally and tell me to get the hell out of there.

"My sail and propeller are – "

Mr. Customs, quivering with unexplained rage, ordered me to arrange a tow with a government tug and to get around the island to English Harbour. The tow, he said, was going to cost me $500 U.S.

I should have had enough sense to go there in the first place; it is a world-reknowned yacht basin. I'd been anxious to push the boat no farther than necessary, and English Harbour was about twenty miles down the coast, around the island's south side.

Mr. Customs' assistant, a local pilot known as "Sweet," told me on the sly he could get me towed for only $300. So the next day, a thirty-five-foot power cruiser called *Octopussy* threw me a line and towed me around to English Harbour. It was a beautiful ride. At the end of it, I peeled off $300 and gave it to two of Sweet's cronies, who roared off in their Chris-Craft whooping and singing.

I took the dinghy ashore in search of a boatyard. Poor, forlorn *Serenity* was bobbing at anchor in the midst of a hundred luxury yachts of all designs and sizes, all of them dwarfing her. A Canadian flag flew from the stump of the mast, qualifying her as a member, albeit a crippled and tiny one, of this international fleet. The sooner I got her repaired the sooner I could sell her.

Sentiment aside, it was clear that my gamble on this boat had been a losing one. Perhaps it *had* been irresponsible to take off on this mad journey. Perhaps it was time to admit that *Serenity* couldn't take it and neither could I. I told myself I wasn't going to miss her and that it didn't matter that I wasn't going to sail around the world after all. I'd enjoy being back in the business world I knew so well and in which I moved so certainly. I told myself all these things. And I knew they were lies.

CHAPTER SEVEN

*R*EAL MEN DON'T CRY. REAL MEN GET DRUNK, LAUGH, TELL LIES, AND GET LAID, BUT MEN CERTAINLY don't cry.

So I held back my tears that April evening, as I walked out of the lawyer's office. I sat in my car, staring unseeing at the city skyline. The document, stapled at the upper left-hand corner through a blue paper triangle, was signed by Wanda and me, our signatures punctuated by two tiny red seals.

Behind the polite recitations of "whereases, notwithstandings, heretofores," and the flurry of signatures were our "irreconcilable differences" and agreement to go our separate ways. The paper gave Wanda everything except my company shares, some paintings, my sports equipment, and my two mistresses: the bicycle and *Serenity IV*. Mine, too, was an emotional wrenching from the relationship through which all our joys, dreams, sorrows, achievements, and aspirations had been channelled. I was now officially cut off from a way of life, a family, comfortable habits, and a wife of twenty-nine years. True, I had gradually severed myself from these things by taking up residence in the hotel and living on my boat, but a legal document now existed that gave it all substance and finality.

As I started the car I found myself pretending. Against all reason, I told myself that what I had signed wasn't really a separation agreement, merely an insurance policy to protect my family from prolonged probate should I be lost at sea. But my lies were transparent: I felt hollow and beaten.

I had arrived back from the Caribbean a month earlier, leaving *Serenity*, mastless and at anchor, in English Harbour. I was quite disoriented; I should have been at sea, not back in

Toronto. I had put my everyday life in a holding pattern and it was a joyless chore reactivating it. I had made it known that I would be unavailable for consulting work and the mortgage market was flat. There was little work I wished to do and no landbound challenges attracted me.

I'd made an abortive effort to rekindle my marriage: I cabled Wanda from Antigua and asked her to meet me in Florida. I don't know what I expected Delray Beach to do for us, but the pragmatism in me said, "Let's give it a try." I was trying to come to terms with the disappointment of my truncated voyage. Within a week we flew back to Toronto. I reluctantly picked up the threads of my business life, out of habit and necessity. It would take very little for me to cast off the burden.

My release came with a phone call!

I'd sawed off the jagged end of my broken mast and sent it to a metallurgy lab. Since the accident, I'd assumed that the fracture was due to metal fatigue. I thought that the constant whipping of the spar had caused it to break, much as a piece of wire can snap after being bent back and forth repeatedly. I had expected nothing more from the laboratory than a confirmation of my assumption, and I was already devising a new method of construction.

I almost choked with surprise when the lab reported that the metal was sound and had not suffered from the abuse it had taken in the open ocean. The reason for the break was absurdly, maddeningly simple. When rigging the mast, the St. Catharines yard had had to fasten a winch, cleats, and a pad eye, and to cut an exit opening for the halyard about four feet above the deck. They had drilled all the holes on the same horizontal plane, weakening the mast by about sixty per cent at that point. Naturally, it had snapped!

The news melted my self-pity and apathy. *Serenity* was *not* at fault: she and I had been the victims of circumstances; far from being dead in the water, *Serenity* had been wounded only, by the mistakes of her outfitters. The journey was not over!

If there had been any hope for reconciliation with Wanda during these few weeks, I think this is where it ended. My undisguised joy at the prospect of putting to sea again dashed whatever remained of Wanda's goodwill. Within days I was back in a hotel room; but my myopic state of mind was such that I didn't brood about our relationship at all, or about what was happening to me. Every waking moment was getting me closer to *Serenity* and the sea. Wanda and I consulted in the tartly civilized way couples do when love is guttering like a neglected candle. It was during one of those conversations that we decided to draw up a paper that would allow her and the children to have access to my estate should I disappear at sea. It was a short step from that talk to a separation agreement.

It would take more than two months to outfit *Serenity* with a new mast and rigging from George Hinterhoeller's yard. He had accepted responsibility for the damage and replaced the mast, rigging, and wishbone at his expense.

I was also provided with a new sail. I worked with the designer to eliminate the roach, battens, and any other inland water design features that could be incompatible with the stress and abuses of a blue-water passage. The sail-maker assured me that it would have all the strength and durability that I needed.

Again, I spent hours scouring through libraries, catalogues, and shops for charts and sailing instructions, covering almost every possible destination in the Southern Hemisphere I could choose on my forthcoming departure from Antigua. The North Atlantic was already well covered.

During the time that wasn't taken up with dreaming, planning, and sailing preparations, I found myself transported back in time on Bay Street. Work had a comfortable familiarity to it, yet I felt disassociated from it. Joan Hammell had things running so smoothly that I often felt redundant; so by early afternoon, I'd usually find myself inventing errands, trudging around the teeming downtown canyons in the brisk spring breeze. On every corner there were reminders of past business ventures. Other memories took me back to Madison Avenue or Sixth, Grosvenor Street, and St. James's; but downtown Toronto was where I had cut my business teeth.

"Coming in second doesn't count." "There is no such word as can't."

94

1941, when *Pristis* cost sixty dollars and a few hundred hours of hard work. Next came *Canuck*, a beautiful 25-footer sold in 1952 (inset).

As President of Triton Centres Ltd., I was riding high on the success of Yorkdale and of hosting HRH Princess Alexandra (inset) on a royal tour of the Shopping Centre.

(above) CEO of the locker room in 1959. We had few wins, but lots of spirit. In the second row are my son Stephen (third from left) and John Barker, my crew on the St. Lawrence (second from right).

Wonderful trade winds and
glorious sunshine south
of Antigua; then noon
sextant sights in the
Doldrums (inset).

Terror in the North Atlantic: the jury-rigged mast stump (inset above) and Irving (inset left), the fastest bowels between the Azores and Bermuda.

Heady speed under challenging conditions in the South Atlantic ended a few days later with a ripped sail at the masthead (inset above) and a distress flag above the deck (inset left).

MV *Masirah* brings rescue and a new life. Top: (left) Chief Officer Andy Pritchard, "What can we do for you?" (right) Will and Rosemary Headon, offering friendship, sandwiches and charm. Middle: (left) Captain Polson, Master of the *Masirah*. (right) Chief Tim Read, engine room and five million frozen chickens. Bottom: Second Officer Rob Brindle, inventor of the nautical banana, who first sighted *Serenity*.

Very early, my parents made clear that success was my birthright. I was to wear the mantle of responsibility with the ease and stature of one to the manor born. Their confidence created a self-fulfilling prophecy, and, quite simply, I succeeded at everything I attempted. Sports, school work, social relationships, and the accumulation of money all seemed to come easily, with what appeared to be minimum effort.

In actual fact, however, I was very selective in the arenas in which I elected to play out the games – choosing only those in which I could win. This may account for the lack of defeats, but it also must have allowed me to concentrate all of my efforts on those endeavours that would result in ultimate victory.

As a youngster I assumed I would head my class and did, until university, where I met much stiffer competition. Here I never resolved the contest as I was forced by a family financial crisis to leave in the middle of my third year to get a paying job. My brother was already out in the world and between the two of us we helped maintain a strong and happy family.

After a few years in the work force I fell madly in love with, what else, the most beautiful girl in the world! Nothing would do but I would build her a house.

In 1948 I had little money to spare while helping to support our family on Toronto Island. I worked as a draftsman in a small architectural office downtown. There was, however, something I coveted. On the Island, at the corner of the Boardwalk and Pontiac Avenue, there was a vacant lot, from which you could look north at the Toronto skyline and south over Lake Ontario to the clouds rising over Niagara Falls.

All residential property on the Island was rented on twenty-year leases. I arranged the necessary documents – without a lawyer – and became the proud twenty-year tenant of a fifty-foot by one-hundred-sixty-foot piece of sand and scrub, barely protected from the furies of Lake Ontario by a hopelessly inadequate break wall and the famous Boardwalk. The ten dollars a month land rent was eked out from overtime pay.

I designed an 800-square-foot bungalow, secured my building permit, opened accounts with various building supply houses, and commenced work on my own, calling on the sometimes willing labour of family and friends. By April I put the ceremonial shovel in the ground – a borrowed garden spade – and started mixing concrete with a hoe on an old piece of plywood. With the foundation in, my lack of experience did not stop me from completing the floor, wall, and roof construction – all done with hand tools during the hours of fading daylight, after a full day's work in the drafting room.

By August, my creditors were beginning to make uneasy noises since I had yet to write a cheque, and I entered what would be my spiritual home for the next thirty years: Bay Street. Every noon-hour for days, I looked for a bank or trust company, anyone who would lend me the money I needed. Finally, Messrs. Sinclair, Goodenough, Higginbottom & McDonald, Barristers and Solicitors, took back a mortgage on my yet to be completed house: $3,000 at $3^3/_4$ per cent over ten years.

I did not realize it at the time, but I had just been initiated into the world of the land developers. Although still a neophyte, I had learned to design and build as economically as possible, to use suppliers' money, to borrow the maximum at the minimum rate for the longest term, and above all, to tie up as little of my own money as possible.

The house was finished in thirteen months, in time for my marriage. Out of a salary of $38.50 a week, I paid a mere $112.50 a year interest and $14.80 a month for land rent and taxes. Who could ask for a more favourable cash flow?

Clearly, there was no future for me in architectural drafting, and I knew I would never be more than an mediocre designer; so I joined a small general contractor as general superintendent. After a few low bids, I found myself sharing my desk with the receivers: the company was bankrupt.

I had one child with another on the way. At twenty-five years old, I was having my first taste of losing. Fear gripped me with an intensity I had never felt before. Days of calling on contractors and architects did nothing to ease my anxiety. Then I made a five-cent call from a phone booth at the southwest corner of Adelaide and Yonge Streets, which was to land me on my feet and establish the course of my business future.

A new type of entrepreneur, the "owner-builder," was appearing. The Yellow Pages listed three: Commercial Industrial Leaseholds in Hamilton and Toronto Industrial Leaseholds and Principal Investments, both in Toronto. Principal was only two blocks away, so I called them. I had no professional qualifications, but I had gall and enough experience in architecture and construction to spin a good story.

With both a design and construction staff under the same roof the Bennett brothers of Principal Investments were just starting, in 1952, to build things called "shopping centres." My qualifications meshed with their requirements, and I was made assistant to Eph Diamond. A few years my senior, Eph was an engineering and business graduate from Queen's. He taught me the little then known about the fledgling shopping-centre business and then left to form his own development company, which later became the giant Cadillac-Fairview Corporation. Under Eph's direction I supervised construction of Toronto's very first shopping centre: Sunnybrook Plaza, at Bayview and Eglinton.

Developers from all over North America and Europe came to view the opening of our next centre, Lawrence Plaza, in 1954. It was the largest project I'd ever managed – a $2 million investment – and absorbed all of my waking hours: designing, constructing, redesigning, finding money, holding off creditors, and working with tenants and prospective users of space who did not really understand what was happening. We were inventing the business as we went along.

I learned, and quickly, not only about construction, but about leasing, financing, real estate, and bankruptcy laws, a cumulation of endless details that separate a good developer from a bad one and motivate tenants and bankers alike to part with their money for future profits.

Lawrence Plaza was just the beginning and by 1957, while still an employee, I had made a name for myself as an expert in shopping centres – if only by virtue of quantity alone: Montreal, Ottawa, Sudbury, Kitchener, Windsor, Regina, Calgary, Edmonton, and a dozen more.

The company was just beginning to sniff around the U.S. Midwest and New York State when competition arrived on the local scene: William Zeckendorf.

After trying to improve my position with the Bennett brothers, whom I admired and respected, I realized I had plateaued. It was time to capitalize on my unique experience and go for the "big money."

I was completing Principal Investments' North Hill Shop-

ping Centre in Calgary and, on a piece of Wales Hotel station-
ery, I wrote a "To Whom It May Concern" letter to impress
upon Mr. Zeckendorf that certain disaster would face Webb &
Knapp if it failed to hire North America's most brilliant young
shopping centre entrepreneur. Humility was not one of my
virtues. Besides, it would not get me into the office of a high
roller like William Zeckendorf!

I hit pay dirt: $12,000 per annum, the title of assistant vice-
president, and the responsibility for all of Webb & Knapp's
retail developments. A year or so later I was a full vice-
president in charge of a dozen developments, wheeling and
dealing from Halifax to Vancouver. One of my major responsibilities, and a thorn in my side, was the presidency of Toronto
Industrial Leaseholds, which Webb & Knapp came to control.
TIL had approximately ninety subsidiary companies, all insol-
vent.

Here I learned my bankruptcy law well. As director of record
I was served writs at home with such regularity that Wanda
and the sheriff's representatives had coffee together in our
kitchen three or four times a week.

By 1960, when the labyrinthine affairs of Zeckendorf began
to crumble, I'd built a reputation as a golden boy. In innumer-
able photographs of ribbon cuttings, cornerstone layings, and
civic receptions there was David Philpott, front and centre,
sporting an immodest smile, a rich tan, expensive suit, and
that air of vitality and confidence that comes only from
youthful success in the fast lane.

When Zeckendorf's Webb & Knapp went under, he and his
Madison Avenue office survived, but his empire had to be
drastically restructured. Colleagues who'd seemed secure
found themselves on the street. But not me. I was a winner,
and I intended to keep on winning.

Out of the rubble of Webb & Knapp (Canada) Limited
(which continued to operate while its American parent faced
bankruptcy litigation) emerged Trizec. "Tri" stood for the
three partners: "Z" for Zeckendorf, "E" for Eagle Star Insurance of London, England, and "C" for Covent (Canada)
Limited, a subsidiary of Covent Garden Properties Limited of
London.

It was a solid, well-financed holding company controlled by

"the English," as we called them. I was made CEO and president of its development subsidiary, Triton Centres Limited. At thirty-four years old I was flush with my own successes: a safety deposit box full of stock options and a company of my own to run. Triton was the greatest joy and the blackest disappointment of my business career. It also made my personal fortune and provided my toughest challenges.

The greatest challenge was Yorkdale Shopping Centre in Toronto. Yorkdale is not an exceptional development by today's standards, but in 1960 we were pioneers: this was to be the largest retail project in the world. After almost five years of intensive negotiations, government obstruction, rejection by banks, design and construction difficulties, and resistance from retailers it emerged as the most innovative commercial real estate project in North America. I can still call it a "triumph" without feeling awkward, and there is more of me in it than anything else I have done. Yorkdale opened in 1964 and, due partially to the lack of competitive developments, garnered the huge, booming market of northwest Metropolitan Toronto. As Yorkdale took off, I started to make real money for the first time in my life.

I loved it: the power, status, prestige, and all the things that money could buy. But most of all I was addicted to winning. I had been brought up to come first and my life had proved it was my right.

Like my father before me, however, I discovered that success is transient and authority vulnerable. By 1970, the power merchants with whom I shared boardrooms in three countries began to shift uneasily and choose up sides. In a protracted corporate power struggle, I found myself on the losing team. Although I remained on Trizec's board of directors, gradually I was stripped of executive powers and found myself clearing out my desk on the evening of December 31, 1972.

I was alone in the office when I heard a noise in the reception area. It was Bill Laird, a lawyer I had met years earlier when I was negotiating shopping-centre leases for the Bennetts. Laird used to work for Loblaw's and had resigned under circumstances similar to mine ten years earlier. He had been on his own ever since. He spent an hour or more telling me his story, and in those sixty minutes he took me from the depths of depression to a buoyancy and optimism that has seldom left me. Laird understood what it meant to be forced to cut the ties with the company I had helped to build for fifteen years. He knew it was an emotional wrench and a blow to my pride that would leave scars.

On September 30, I had given the Trizec board of directors three months' notice of my intentions to resign. During those months I was a pariah; those who supported me would do so surreptitiously for fear of reprisals. Others were openly contemptuous of my lame-duck status. It was an extremely difficult time but one that contributed a great deal to my business and personal maturity and honed my executive and human-relations abilities to a fine edge.

I began 1973 by throwing off the corporate shackles. My talk with Bill Laird, a relative stranger who took time on New Year's eve to help me face up to the crisis, was a unique experience I will not soon forget. I stepped out into the world, like the cocky kid I'd been in my youth, and incorporated a company of my own.

CHAPTER EIGHT

I HAD MADE MY DECISION. *I WOULD CIRCUMNAVIGATE THE WORLD SINGLE-HANDED.* THE LAZILY SPINNING vanes of the overhead fan sent out a pinwheel of shadows across the walls of my room in the "Copper and Lumber Store," the hotel I'd chosen on my return to Antigua. It was a comfortable, two-level apartment, lovingly restored, with old oak plank floors aromatic with wax, bright-beamed ceilings, and a beautifully crafted wooden staircase joining the sitting room and the bedroom. Still, it might have been an old packing box for all I cared. I felt imprisoned, out of my element, seething with impatience.

Why this impatience? Why the compulsion to cross oceans and make extended passages alone? I had time to question my motives – even my sanity. I had read that many such sailors are just plain crazy or suffer from emotional disorders; and, no doubt, a few single-handers have had mental problems. Single-handed sailors are certainly not "normal" in the sense that the average person hasn't the inclination, or perhaps the nerve, to emulate them; but, contrary to views of many of my pin-striped colleagues on Bay Street, most open-ocean single-handers are completely sane.

Dr. John C. Lilly, a noted psychoanalyst-sailor, made a study of single-handers and wrote forthrightly: "A mentally ill person by definition can't successfully cross an ocean single-handed." Yet solo voyages certainly have been completed by men and women not playing with a full deck, while others have not succeeded, because of circumstances completely unrelated to their state of mind.

In my reading I came across various explanations of why a sailor would attempt single-handing: "to prove to myself that I could do it alone"; "recklessness was nagging me"; "to test myself and my independence"; "because I bloody well wanted to."

As for my reasons, I really did not know, except that I had an uncontrollable drive to change the direction of my life. It was essential that I seek new reasons and experiences that would enrich and broaden the world before me.

In *The Ulysses Factor*, J.R.L. Anderson writes that there is an exploring instinct in man, derived, for the most part, from the primitive need to discover, pioneer, have adventures, investigate, and satisfy curiosity through physical effort. Anderson theorizes all men have the Ulysses factor to some extent; but in modern times, there are few frontiers left to explore. The instinct is often strong in fliers, mountain climbers, and offshore sailors, especially solo voyagers; and it is better satisfied through individual achievement than through large-scale team effort.

Richard Henderson points out that most solo voyagers probably share what might be called a romantic optimism, an idealistic outlook that allows them to make light of bad times: the gales, hardships, fatigue, loneliness, worries, and fear. The single-hander thinks mainly of scudding before the trade winds with warm sun on his back, his dream ship sliding off before foam-flecked seas of the deepest blue. He also dreams of landfalls on tropic isles with palm-fringed lagoons and native girls bedecked with flowers.

I didn't particularly agree with Dr. John Lilly or Messrs. Anderson and Henderson; but I did know that David Philpott intended to be the first Canadian to circle the globe single-handed via the Clipper route. For the sheer joy of it!

When I was in Antigua three and a half months earlier, I certainly was not feeling like a romantic adventurer. Anything but! I had contacted a local yacht broker, as *Serenity IV* had unquestionably proven herself totally incapable of handling offshore conditions. The broker offered me no encouragement. The boat had little chance of being sold in Antigua. He suggested I take it to St. Thomas, where I would find a much better market. And that is exactly what I had intended to do, as soon as I had restored the mast and put *Serenity* in sailing condition.

Before returning to Toronto I shipped five cartons – 450

pounds – of personal effects and gear that would not be included with the boat if she were sold. I was bitter. *Serenity IV* was nothing more than a broken toy, anchored in Falmouth Bay amidst a huge fleet of *real* yachts from all over the world. She wasn't up to it; *Serenity* was out of her class.

I had called Mr. Simmonds, who ran the local boatyard, and we arranged that as soon as the mast was shipped to him he would proceed with the installation.

Among the taxi drivers who competed aggressively and sometimes angrily for business around English Harbour I selected Ephram. After negotiating a flat rate to St. John's we established quite a friendship, and he drove me almost daily to the airline, telephone, and freight offices and often took me up to a lookout on the mountain, where I saw all of the island's south shore spread below. It became apparent why Lord Nelson, and many fleets before him, had found this a safe haven from both enemies and the weather.

Mr. Simmonds, who must have had a first name but held out for "Mister," would not allow any boat to be left in his yard unless someone on the island was responsible for it – and Ephram was my man. He would look after the boat, keep it clean, protect it from vandals, and sand and oil the teak bright-work for $100 U.S. per month.

Serenity was for sale. March 21 was to be my last night onboard unless I moved her to St. Thomas. I had spent twenty-two days and nights alone on the ocean, and I had enjoyed every one of them. I regretted that I would probably never again experience that delicious insecure sensation of sleeping while the boat took over, moving us both through unknown waters to tomorrow. Would I ever wake up again to check the log to see what progress I had made during the night, and the compass to see if we were still on course? All of these things I would miss. Never again would I take a noon sun sight, pour over my charts and tables, plot, calculate, and navigate for endless hours. Never again would I eat silly meals, go to bed shortly after sundown, and rise at dawn with that idyllic feeling of solitude that is so beautifully unique to the single-handed sailor.

On March 22 I flew to Fort Lauderdale, and a few days later to Toronto and what I thought was to be the reconstruction of

103

my life. My little company, now grown to an almost dull level of profitability eight years after its incorporation, absorbed my time but not my soul.

Until that phone call – that magnificent, wonderful phone call, telling me the mast was sound! Then I knew: *Serenity* and I would go for it!

Now, almost four months later, in mid-July, I had landed at the St. John's airport. I struggled and cajoled my 400 pounds through Antiguan customs knowing that *Serenity* still wasn't ready for me. David Simmonds (we were on a first-name basis now) of Antigua Shipways had warned me, when I phoned from Toronto on the only line to English Harbour, that the boat hadn't even been moved to dockside, so it couldn't be hooked up to shore power. Besides, I had stripped her of everything in the way of cooking utensils and food when I thought of selling.

So, here I was in the "Copper and Lumber Store," brooding.

Despite Simmonds' warning I couldn't resist a visit to the boatyard on my arrival. There I found *Serenity* bobbing at anchor exactly where I'd left her more than three months earlier, with the butt of her mast still sticking up like a rude gesture.

Antiguan bureaucrats decided that I would have to clear the new mast sail and gear through customs in person. It would be a day or two before I'd be able to talk to the right officials, and Simmonds had no idea when they'd release the shipment, let alone how soon the work would be completed. He was kind and sympathetic, but quite content with the relaxed pace of the island. Now that the owner was here, of course, the work would proceed more quickly; but only as quickly as was necessary to satisfy the demands of courtesy.

Instead of taking the opportunity to unwind and enjoy the pleasures of the island, I found myself more than willing to trade a week of this languid life for one telephone-ringing, deal-making, pressured, tension-filled day at the office. This startled me, because I'd come to believe that I'd put all that behind me. Not far enough, apparently. I was not moving, and moving seemed to be an essential ingredient of my life. I wouldn't wait in line for a movie or to shake hands with God Himself, and here I was stowed away on this rusty tropical isle.

104

To be fair to Simmonds, the bulk of the work couldn't be done without the equipment I had brought or the mast, sail, and other components still in customs. He was well aware that I wanted to be away before the beginning of the hurricane season, a few weeks away; but if I was distracted and irritated by the interminable delays, that was my problem, not his.

One of the first matters I had to clear up was the matter of my "boat-sitter." Although Ephram had given every indication of being an upstanding, responsible citizen and had thoroughly disarmed me during our rides around the island, he had a rogue within. Simmonds informed me that Ephram had sub-contracted the work to a shy young man named Roland – for only fifty dollars a month – and was sixty days in arrears. By the time I reached English Harbour, Simmonds was paying the duped Roland from the money I had sent the Slipways on account. Ephram and my money were nowhere to be found. I learned later he was in jail.

After settling accounts with Roland, I started to load *Serenity* with all the marine gear that I had brought from Toronto. This meant rowing between the boat and the dock in my Avon inflatable dinghy, which Roland had kept on shore for me. It is a cruel irony that, after planning a major ocean voyage, with all of its dangers and tests of seamanship, I would dump the dinghy. Crueller still, I dumped twice. I did little damage other than destroying a Hewlett Packard calculator into which I had laboriously inserted a program to assist me in navigation.

After weeks of research, trigonometric calculations, and formulae, I had distilled complex sight reductions to the pressing of a few buttons. It had been a fascinating exercise, designed to save time and increase efficiency. Three hundred Xeroxed computer forms were dumped into an English Harbour trash can, symbolizing my return to basics and a rejection of high-tech navigation.

Other than this minor mishap the fitting-out process went well. I changed the oil, organized my new equipment, and re-examined the electrical and mechanical systems as well as the integrity of the hull and other structural components.

Then there was the problem of food for the voyage.

Going it alone, I had an advantage over a crewed vessel: I did not have to carry a great quantity of food. Nevertheless, I prudently figured that I would take longer to reach my destination than a fully crewed boat would; and it was absolutely essential that I be adequately nourished. Even with vitamin pills and nutrition supplements, there is a danger of ill health from a steady diet of canned food.

Refrigeration was impractical because of its electrical demand. There are, however, nourishing foods that will keep for long periods without ice: nuts, cheese, macaroni, beans, rice, lentils, cereals, granola. Margarine, eggs, and dried fruit will last, but for only a limited time in the tropics. Fresh meat was impossible but I intended to rely primarily on powdered or canned milk, and tins of meat and poultry for animal protein. Fish would be available, of course, but many varieties are toxic, and my unhappy experience with a flying-fish dinner earlier in the voyage made me wary of relying on the sea as a source of food.

One half gallon per man per day is the rule of thumb for fresh water, and I had seventy gallons, almost twice the amount required for the three-month voyage.

Needless to say I had researched all of this thoroughly and had prepared a list of provisions that would be stowed according to a consumption schedule – all in the best traditions of order, common sense, and good seamanship.

Roland drove me to St. John's, where outsiders fight for goods and services with the local citizens. My arena was the local supermarket, the only substantial source of food in town. The store was huge, but the shelves were all but empty.

There was no variety or choice, and most items were "temporarily out of stock." I shifted mental gears and a revised list of provisions for an eighty-day open-sea voyage was conceived on the floor of the St. John's Supermart. Campbell's chunky soups, a big feature on my original list, were nowhere to be seen. Instead I bought canned and dried products of questionable origin, which I correctly suspected would have little or no solid content. Otherwise, food from the store's meagre pickings I found good. Eighty days' groceries were heavy on canned fruit and juices, hot and cold cereals, and enough powdered milk to make eighty quarts. The rest of the larder was made up of many tins of meat of unknown persuasion from Denmark, Italy, and Austria. Yet the consequences of my shopping expedition were surprisingly adequate and were to satisfy my needs for the entire voyage.

Over several days I ferried the supplies out to *Serenity*, but with the oppressive heat of the Antiguan summer beating me down, even this little effort left me wrung out. The temperature was well in excess of 110°F. I would manage two loads a day, with a shower in between, then collapse in exhaustion. I finally smartened up and did the work when the sun went down. Characteristically, I learned the value of the midday siesta the hard way.

Although I was working reasonably hard, I had no desire to eat. In the four days since I had arrived, I'd had one plate of bacon and eggs, two cups of coffee, and gallons, literally gallons, of fruit juice and water. I did buy a loaf of bread and put it in a kitchen drawer in my apartment; but when I went to get it, a big ugly bug had already gnawed through the crust and was well on his way to tunnelling to the other end. That took care of the bread and any temptation to economize by housekeeping.

Even now, that beasty and other creatures with whom I shared the apartment are grim in my memory. One evening I was reading Eric Hiscock, who had far more lyrical memories of Antigua than I would retain, when my elbow brushed the window drapes. A great furry spider bounced off my left ear and landed, all six legs at the ready, on the open page. I froze. He cleared his bowels on the paper and began to ease his way slowly over toward my bare knee. I shot up as if I'd been in an ejector seat; book and bug landed on the floor about ten feet in front of me. Quickly, far too quickly, I stepped on him.

Now, squashing insects underfoot is a common North American custom, even a ritual. But sandwiching a furry spider the size of a chipmunk between your Adidas and the floor and transferring onto it your full body weight is an unforgettable experience. The noise alone was enough to turn the stomach of a slaughterhouse worker. The spider's remains ended up in the toilet; I was in a cold sweat. I couldn't wait to be gone. And the work seemed to be taking forever.

These bleak moods came and went, driven by the pace and problems of the moment. During the heat of the day, when work was impossible, I would talk to the shop owners and street vendors, and generally play tourist. Often I would end up at an open-air restaurant and watch the fishermen unloading their catch. The waitresses were also a catch, and we became more provocative with each passing day. I was single, or almost. Ella would get my juices flowing as she flounced off to the kitchen sending unmistakable signals. I squeezed a lime into my drink and thought pleasant thoughts.

The summer of 1945 was hot and wonderful. I had earned seven firsts out of a possible nine in my departmental exams, which assured me entry into the School of Architecture at the University of Toronto. I had a beautiful girlfriend with whom I had been deeply in love for at least six days. My brother and I had bought an old boat, just crying to be put into racing trim. The war in Europe was over, and Mr. Truman had just dropped two atomic bombs on Japan.

My father, who had been publisher of *Liberty* magazine during the 1930s, had, after weathering the Depression, lost his money through unfortunate investments early in the war. My brother, two sisters, and mother were moved from our eighteen-room house in Rosedale to a cottage on Ward's Island, where we had spent the winter sealing windows and unfreezing pipes. When we moved to a larger home on the lakeshore the following spring, much of the pressure had lifted off my parents. Life was returning to a stripped-down form of normalcy. Most important, the world was waiting for me.

This was my summer for big money! I was the local iceman. I had the ice delivered in two-hundred-pound blocks to the Ward's Island dock. I cut it into fifty-pound units and hauled about half a ton in a two-wheeled, hand-drawn wagon. I had about 120 customers daily. Granted, I had to kick in my share to help support the family, but there was enough money left over to provide me, by 1945 standards, with the "good life."

The cicadas were singing, the elms and willow leaves looked late-summer dusty, there was a rainbow ring around the sun, and you could tell it was August. My first load had been delivered and I was back on the dock at about nine-thirty in the morning carving up the huge slabs with my ice tongs and pick. The blocks were carefully piled into the wagon with most of the weight at the rear, so all I had to do was pull the balanced rig without wasting energy. After a thousand pounds had been loaded and covered with a tarpaulin, the remaining pile of ice, still on the dock, was shaded by two layers of heavy canvas. I was off on my second run of the morning with a wonderful feeling that life could not possibly be better.

Although I knew most of my customers, I very seldom saw them. They would buy tickets – one for every twenty-five pounds – and these green tags would be left stuffed in the screen door indicating the exact amount needed in the ice box. I would merely unlatch the top compartment of the refrigerator, shift the old ice to one side, and slip in the required block, taking the tickets with me as I left. On occasion one of the ladies might be in the kitchen and we would exchange pleasantries.

This morning, however, was different. I was about halfway through my load and the pulling was getting easier as I approached a customer's house, a little larger and better appointed than most of the residences on the lakeshore. Usually "Mrs. Robinson" (with apologies to Mike Nichols) took fifty pounds. I clamped a block in my tongs and started for the back door.

Blue jeans had come into fashion a few years earlier. We wore them with the cuffs turned up twice to show a generous length of thick cotton sweatsock buried in a pair of dirty running shoes. I wore no shirt, just glistening sweat and a tan; my pants were soaked with ice water from the hips to the cuffs. The ice hanging from the tongs in my right hand was dripping into my shoe as my left hand reached for the door handle. Locked. I knocked and the door was quickly unlatched. "Mrs. Robinson" was an older woman, all of thirty-five, with long dark hair in the fashion of the day. I knew she had a beautiful figure beneath her dressing gown.

"I've been waiting for you!"

"Why?" I asked with a lilt of curiosity.

"We're going to weigh ice this morning."

"I beg your pardon?"

"We're going to see if fifty pounds of ice weighs fifty pounds, and if it doesn't your going to get paid for just what you deliver."

I was flustered, but still in control. "I'm sure it won't weigh fifty pounds. It's been melting since I cut it up at the dock."

"That's your problem. Let's get it in here and see what I am getting for my money." I carried the dripping ice across the kitchen floor, through the front hall, and up the stairs to the bathroom. It was a large room with 1920s fixtures, the walls covered with rectangular white tiles crazed with the finest of grey cracks. The floor was a grey battleship linoleum and a set of bathroom scales sat in the middle.

"Here," she said.

I carried my melting block across to the scale, losing ounces by the second as the ice water made a river from the door to the threatening instrument on the floor. I placed the narrow end of the block on the scales and stepped back.

"Get those tongs."

I quickly removed the five-pound tongs and leaned over to look at the scale. Thirty-eight pounds and a few ounces! Before she could say anything I went on the offensive. "I told you it wouldn't measure up. It's 85° out there and I'm losing ice water by the gallon from the moment I leave the dock."

"Did you ever see the old picture of this house when my father used to live here?"

I couldn't believe what I was hearing. No tirade, no demand that I charge her less, no screaming that she was sick and tired of being fleeced by tradesmen. Just a silly question.

"Well, have you?"

"No, but I would like to." Anything to keep the conversation away from what I considered to be a losing business encounter. She motioned me out of the room ahead of her, the thirty-eight-pound block of ice still sitting on the bathroom scales, and directed me to a closed door, which led to a large bedroom at the front of the house overlooking the lake. She closed the door and went over to a table covered with a dozen or so framed photographs, some of their sepia tones barely visible. She picked up the largest frame from the rear of the collection and held up a picture of the house. It looked no different than a view from the boardwalk that very day. A closer look, however, revealed a bearded man in shirt sleeves with a black jacket draped over his right arm, a derby hat fitting squarely on his head.

"That's Daddy. He loved this house and the garden."

"Yes, it looks very nice. When was the picture taken?" I felt I had to keep this thing going or she would get back to the block of ice.

110

"In 1912, I was just a baby then, but they say I played over there on that end of the porch." I was beginning to worry about the rest of my thirty-eight-pound ice blocks, which were getting lighter by the minute out on the sidewalk. I edged towards the door, thanking her for showing me the picture and assuring her that I would make sure she got a "bigger" fifty-pound block in the future. She slipped quickly over toward the door and put her hand on my shoulder. "You're all hot and perspiry. Here, let me towel you off and give you a cold drink."

I was obviously missing the thrust of this whole play as my mind was still on the load of ice that had yet to be delivered. I could see my profits melting away.

"No, thank you very much, but I have a lot of customers out there who are still waiting."

Now to this day, all I remember is staring at bare breasts, pubic hair, at least one navel, and a red-rimmed, perfectly round mouth with the tip of a very wet tongue moving slowly around its circumference. She was on the bed. I was trembling and getting a headache. I had been fantasizing about such situations all through puberty, and here it was!

I suddenly felt the cold clammy wetness of my jeans and the water in my right shoe. It made a squishing sound as I shifted weight. I mumbled politely as I exited into the upstairs hall and down the front stairs. Instinct stopped me dead at the bottom. I raced back into the bathroom, retrieved my ice tongs, and was out of the back door in seconds.

That was half of my experience of raw sex during my teens. The second was with a divorcee in Chilliwack, B.C., where I had been sent by the Canadian Officers' Training Corps of the university. The experience was almost identical.

After a few more years of groping, grunting, and grasping in dark strange places to the sound of heavy breathing and the pain of a groin aching with frustration, I entered married life in 1950 with all the outward appearances of a philanderer, lecher, libertine, and rake, but in reality a very unworldly virgin.

What did she do with thirty-eight pounds of ice melting on her bathroom floor?

I had done all I could to prepare for the voyage. I had made intricate lists of supplies and schematics of their location. I had stowed my provisions according to a written plan and diagram, by number and sequence, so as not to have to eat canned peaches for days until I found the corned-beef hash.

One difficulty in leaving from a small harbour was the lack of equipment available. I very much wanted, and eventually acquired, a second nautical almanac, spare parts for the engine, which I needed for electricity if nothing else, and a second sextant.

During the month prior to leaving Toronto, charts, tables, and all the nautical publications I did not yet own had to be acquired for both sides of the Atlantic. (I had to have the option of choosing safe harbours in Europe, Africa, Central or South America, or even the mid-Atlantic islands.) Oddly, I needed more than 120 charts to get from Toronto to Halifax but only four to get from Antigua to my destination: South Africa.

I had no intention of being locked into a single program, and I made preparations for any and all alternatives, whether dictated by choice, accident, or weather. Time had worked against me, however. If I had been able to leave a few weeks earlier, I could have picked up the classical Clipper route to South Africa, which ran south from the Cape Verde Islands to a point off Rio de Janeiro then on to Capetown along an easy southeasterly arc.

Although the Clipper route is substantially longer than a direct line of travel, it is said to take less time, but I never would get the opportunity to prove it. The track from Antigua to the Cape Verdes would take me north and east; my pilot chart for July indicated that the Atlantic, north of 10° latitude, could expect cyclones any time after July 11. It was now July 19. As Antigua is 18° north of the Equator, I needed a fast 480-mile sail due south before I escaped into the hurricane-free zone.

No sailing the "classical route" for me. By avoiding the impending storms I was committing myself to almost 2,000 miles of beating against winds and currents before I crossed the Equator and picked up the traditional passage through the South Atlantic to Capetown. No clipper ship had ever travelled my route to the Southern Ocean.

In addition to charts and other navigational aids, *Serenity* needed minor adjustments to her equipment and rigging. I strengthened George, my trusty self-steering device, made minor alterations to the plumbing system, added a second halyard to the mast, and, in general, took all proper precautions against the possibility of failure or misfortune.

However, I never lost sight of the fact that I had really had only about three and a half weeks at sea. All of my other sailing experience had been on Lake Ontario and other inland waters. I was still really only a confident, well-educated neophyte on the ocean.

Yet I felt compelled to get to sea as quickly as possible – if only to escape the hazards of land. In addition to my encounter with the great hairy spider, from which I had still not fully recovered, one night I stepped onto the wooden-floored bathroom of my hotel room, when the brother of the cockroach that had eaten my bread a few days earlier nearly tripped me. His lust for life knew no bounds. I flailed at him with bath mats, feet, and towels but he escaped into the woodwork. The preliminary event of the evening was declared a draw.

At two in the morning I was awakened by a thump behind my head on the wall, followed by a second thump on the floor. I turned on the light, and there was a bat as big as a barn owl. Now, if I've got a thing about spiders and bugs, it's nothing to my terror of bats! There it lay, stunned, looking up at me with a face that only its mother could love. I did not have enough killer instinct to step on it as I had the spider, so I turned a wastebasket over top of it. The bat immediately began to flail about inside the container and I knew my night's sleep was done unless I took immediate action.

Even in the early hours of the morning, my survival instincts were honed to a fine point! I took a plastic place mat from the table, slipped it under the overturned wastebasket, and threw all three items – place mat, basket and bat – out the window. The following morning the place mat and wastebasket were still on the front lawn of the hotel as a grim reminder of the battle. The bat had gone. It was time I did, too.

JULY 22:
1320 HOURS:
Serenity IV is now beginning to get some bite into her: the mast was stepped two days ago and the

*wishbone installed. The men worked extra time over
at David Simmonds' yard to get all things in order.
Since tomorrow is Sunday, I will be working alone
and must have that yard work completed or I cannot
proceed with the rigging and other essential items
that are so necessary to speed my departure.*

*The last two and half days have been tough
slogging. It isn't so much the amount of work I have
to do, it's the debilitating heat, which has cut my
production to about fifty per cent. I would go over
and work early in the morning and quit about ten-
thirty, using the remaining hour and a half before
lunch to supervise the work being done by the men. I
am blessed with excellent craftsmen and a good
foreman who is making certain that everything is in
first-class condition.*

I finished the rigging on Sunday; the following day *Serenity*
was hauled out of the water. Four months of tropical vegeta-
tion was scraped off her undersides and a new propeller went
on, along with a coat of bottom paint. *Serenity* was launched
again looking as good, if not better, than that day when I first
saw her bobbing at anchor in Port Credit, light years away.

By 1510 hours on July 23 I had completed the intricate
paperwork prescribed by the Antiguan customs officials and
was taking Barclay Point to the starboard, leaving Falmouth
Bay, Monk's Hill, Shirley Heights, and old Nelson's Dockyard
astern.

Although there had been lots of coming and going in English
Harbour, I created some stir because of the single-sailed catboat rig. At thirty feet, *Serenity* could have served as a dory for
one of those 110-foot luxury yachts that had allowed her to
share their harbour.

I cleared the last customs buoy and rounded the point. At
last I felt the crisp breeze scouring away the muggy air of the
harbour. I smiled at the wisdom of one old salt who, the night
before, had opined that *Serenity* could not sail at all, much
less in the kind of seas that I was going to encounter. That remained to be seen.

CHAPTER NINE

*F*OUR DAYS OUT FROM ANTIGUA.

JULY 27:
1135 HOURS:
I could sense it in my sleep. The change in the
vibrations, the high singing hum, the extra heel to
the boat, and the rattle of the flogging sail. The wind
had increased from force 4 to force 6 and brought
with it a deluge of rain, which I used to shower and
clean off completely.

I'd slept late – it was about 0800 hours – and I went
on deck to find my usual collection of small flying
fish. Serenity *was burying her lee rail and I knew I*
had to shorten sail. I took in one tuck, but the high
wind lasted for only a short time and I shook it out
within a half hour. The sun came out and I am now
sailing under beautiful conditions but bucking into
very high seas, which produce the same conditions
down below I experienced the first day.

After clearing English Harbour I plunged into an immense
and confused sea of "square waves" on a course southeast,
parallelling the coast of South America. Six hundred miles off
my starboard were Venezuela, Guyana, Surinam, and French
Guiana; very shortly on my left would be Senegal, Gambia,
Guinea Bissau, Guinea, Sierra Leone, and Liberia. A few days'
sail, maybe a week or so, could take me to any one of them.
The very fact that it was possible added a touch of romance to
the voyage.

After tending to George and fine-tuning the sail, I unsnapped my safety harness and ventured below. The cabin was careening about wildly. I had learned to make certain that one hand was always on the boat and my knees bent, resisting the natural impulse to fight the motion. Having been ashore too long, however, I missed my footing and, grabbing for the table on the way down, drove my chest into the corner of my starboard bunk. I was now working under the disadvantage of two broken ribs well taped up, and just a few hours out, with 6,000 miles to go – not an auspicious beginning.

After giving the disinterested Antiguan Harbour Radio operator an incorrect departure course, I settled in at the chart table, wondering casually if pirates would try to track down a thirty-foot sailboat on a non-existent course in the Caribbean, while *Serenity* was headed out into the Atlantic.

The wind direction dictated that I sail close-hauled if I hoped to stick to my rhumb line of 128°, a course that would take me as directly as possible around the eastern shoulder of South America. This was the area of the northeasterly trades, but they insisted on blowing from the east instead; I found myself pounding against both seas and wind instead of enjoying what could have been a comfortable broad reach.

My pilot chart for July showed that I could expect to buck currents with a northwest set at 0.7 to 1.2 knots. This meant that, regardless of my southeastern progress through the water, I would be driven back northwest about twenty miles a day.

I hadn't got my sea legs back, and *Serenity* bobbed and weaved unnervingly. Even after three days, the tough, close-hauled sailing made me wince as the safety harness tugged at my broken ribs.

I was able to take my first noon latitude sight on July 27, and it added to my growing confidence in the sextant. This simplest of sextant sights has been known for centuries. By measuring the angle between the horizon and the sun at the exact moment of noon, that is, when the sun has reached its apex in the sky, the observer can calculate his latitude north or south of the Equator. An accurate timepiece, coupled with more complex formulae, is needed to establish longitude, or to "shoot" the moon, stars, or planets. It always amazes me that with a watch and a sextant, I can locate myself within five miles of my exact position on the ocean.

By midday on July 29, I'd crossed east into a new time zone, Greenwich plus three, and my sights put me 563 miles north of the Equator.

For most of the first five days out of Antigua, I had been barrelling along under full sail; but because of the bucking and pitching on confused and extremely rough seas, I rarely had both hands free for anything but the simplest chores.

I had tried to air out the cabin by leaving the lee portholes and the ceiling hatch open, but I was continuously taking blue water over the bow into the cockpit and cabin. Everything below was damp, the cabin floor shiny with water, and the metal fittings beaded with moisture and filmy with salt. When I woke on the morning of July 30, I found the electrical system completely shorted out. I knew a little calm weather would allow it to dry and cure itself, but it was interesting to speculate on what I'd do if I lost power permanently.

I knew both radios could run on dry-cell batteries, if necessary: I really used them only for occasional time signals. The electrical water pressure system was an unnecessary luxury; I could draw off fresh water from the storage tanks with a foot pump. The bilge could be drained manually, and food could be cooked on the propane stove. Other than my music the only thing I would miss would be the odometer; but if seventeenth-century mariners managed without electricity on this very ocean, I could do the same.

The self-steering mechanism, which had become a second member of the crew, had taken a remarkable amount of strain and was performing beautifully. However, a slight movement in the device showed up an "oil-canning" effect in the transom: the struts securing George to the boat alternately pushed and pulled on the structure, which caused the thick plastic of the transom to bend in and out. Eventually the motion could fracture the hull. I solved the problem by lashing the main shaft of the device to the outer extremities of the transom, which prevented it from shifting from side to side. The problem was solved and the lashings would remain unchanged for the remainder of the trip.

I'd gone through my regular ritual of taking seasick pills and now, seven days out, I had regained my sea legs and was on my own. I ate fitfully, subsisting on fruit and vegetable juices. Solid foods, mostly cereal and canned meat, were taken for nourishment rather than enjoyment.

By sundown the wind had dropped; a light breeze gave slight relief on deck and groped feebly into the damp heat of the cabin below. The winds were skittish and changeable, punctuated by vicious little squalls, and I was up and down, time and again, adjusting the steering vane and trimming sail. What sleep I got was restless and full of grey dreams. Two hours before dawn I gave up, lit my oil lamp, and opened a book.

I was re-reading Naomi James's *At One With The Sea*. It was impossible not to make comparisons, as I would be following her track very closely through most of the South Atlantic and around the Cape of Good Hope. It struck me, too, that with the exception of Joshua Slocum, who cast off at the turn of the century without so much as stopping the paper delivery, single-handed sailors took ceremonial leave of their departure points, the wharf groaning under the weight of weeping and cheering well-wishers for James, Chichester, Rose, and the others.

I was obviously doing it all wrong. My only human contact before leaving Antigua was an argument with a gas dock attendant about how much water I could take aboard. I was grateful for my independence, however, when I read James's accounts of missed rendezvous and fouled communications with the agents of her sponsor, *The Daily Express*. I had no one to answer to but myself.

I did share with other single-handed sailors those occasional blessed moments that only such a solitary and eccentric enterprise could offer. The following night out the quantity and composition of clouds gave the sky mystic drama, and Polaris was just kissing the northern horizon. As I sat in the cockpit, the moon slipped out from between two ranges of shifting, vaporous mountains. The air was soft, and the water danced with phosphorescence. The whole panorama had to be a visual litany between sea and sky.

For hours I sat, musing: about my strengths, which had no doubt brought me here to seek a form of primal combat; and my weaknesses, which had put probably hundreds of miles between me and the nearest living soul to escape from irrelevant values. I was just a man, confused, guilty, and sad; but I had a capacity for joy, for love, and for faith, with which I'd lost touch. Could I even begin to unravel my own mysteries, the skein of priorities and relationships I'd knit over the years that had lately begun to chafe and confine me? That rising moon caressing the water, as *Serenity* glided along, had some magic in it. This was not the first, nor would it be the last time I'd felt its spell.

God and I shared an instant out there on the waters.

The next day, I threw all the ports open to let a gentle wind dry out the electrical system. While the swells were relatively calm, I went for my first swim since leaving Antigua. I fastened my safety harness to fifty feet of main-sheet and tied a second line to my wrist to calm my fear of seeing *Serenity* sail off, with me bobbing helplessly in her broadening wake. (This same concern accounted for the hundred-yard length of floating rope, knotted every five feet, which I dragged astern at all times. If my safety harness failed – I always wore it on deck – I could grab this line in the water. Hanging on at high speeds might have been a problem, but I never had to face it.) I also wore a diving mask so that I could look from side to side, underwater, to see if any ocean beasties were gaining on me.

Fortunately, a tiny squall happened along just as I clambered aboard, so I could shower off in the cool rain, flushing the salt out of little cuts and abrasions that sea water caused to stay open and fester.

That night was busy, with calms, squalls, and wind shifts that are the annoying but integral part of sailing in that part of the ocean. Much good the drying out the day before had been. The damp again insinuated itself everywhere, and I carried more of it into the cabin every time I returned from my all-too-often trips on deck during the night. By noon the next day, my hands and feet had been damp so long they had the texture of wet toilet paper. I was feeling as gloomy as the scudding grey ceiling overhead.

At ocean level, the weather had calmed and I'd fired up the engine to charge the batteries. Over its drone, I heard or imagined sounds I'd never encountered before. It took me some time to stop jumping at every ping and groan.

By 1250 hours, the wind had come up from the south; I swung around onto the starboard tack and made fast the running backstay. George Hinterhoeller had made up one for each side, as I was still concerned that the whipping of the mast might cause metal fatigue. The length of the wishbone boom precluded permanent, fixed stays, but I was able to make-down a movable one on the windward side. As I tended to stay on one heading for extended periods, this was a fine arrangement that made me feel more secure.

I was below when there was a sound like a rifle shot. I emerged to find my brand new cable dragging in the water behind the boat. I immediately brought the port stay forward around the mast, securing it to the starboard deck cleat to replace the stay that lay coiled on the cockpit floor. With field glasses, I could see a pinless shackle hanging from the mast tang: back in English Harbour, I must have neglected to secure the pin in the shackle with a lashing, and it had worked loose during the last few days when it had not been under tension.

JULY 31:

0625 HOURS:

I am now in the fabled Doldrums – not emotionally, but physically.

The British Admiralty's Ocean Passages for the World *reads in part, "the equatorial trough or Doldrums is an area of low pressure situated between the trade winds of the two hemispheres. Characteristic features of this area are light and variable winds alternating with squalls, heavy rain and thunder storms."*

However, Bowditch, the American Practical Navigator, *with its editions going back to 1803, gives me some encouragement: "the eastern part in both Atlantic and Pacific are [sic] wider than the western part. In July and August the belt is centered on about 7° north and is several degrees in width, even at its narrowest point."*

The boat felt tired, listless, and the sea had an oily sheen. The full and hot sun glared off the sail, which wagged ineffectually above me. I made some coffee and, leafing through my *Bowditch*, took some heart from the entry that said the western, or my, part of the Doldrums was the narrow end. In the Doldrums one was almost totally at the mercy of the currents. What winds there were blew light and variable, with squalls that would dash in and deliver a sucker punch now and then. The speed and direction of the currents were by the book, and often against me. There was little point in navigating accurately, except to relieve the boredom. I worked endlessly to squeeze some southward progress out of the on-again-off-again winds, trimming and retrimming the sail, trying to make the squalls and currents get *Serenity* out of the trough.

> *AUGUST 2:*
> *0720 HOURS:*
> *During the two days since I've been here, the boat has acted like a petulant baby. I've really been far busier than I was when I had my wonderful runs in the northeast trades. Day or night, clouds, cat's paws, sudden breezes give false signals that a wind is coming up, and I put to work tuning the rigging and the sail for the big blow. Then it comes from a different direction, at a much reduced strength, and dies in about fifteen minutes.*
> *Last night I came on deck – naked as a flea with the exception of my safety harness, moving lines back and forth and getting absolutely soaked – for winds that never arrived. I finally gave up in the firm and disgusted conviction that the whole system was designed solely to keep me awake.*

The demands of the boat were not the only thing that kept me awake. There was also a sudden invasion of croaking, smelly, web-footed sea birds, which took us for a floating island. They were slightly larger than pigeons with long, downward curving bills, impressive wingspans, and white topknots that stopped just short of their beady eyes, giving them a perpetually furious look.

121

From my bird book I deduced that they were probably Brown-footed Boobies, which range all over the South Atlantic; and never were birds so aptly named. They live at sea and touch shore but once a year to mate. Possibly this was their annual love fest – an orgy would certainly break the monotony.

There must have been two dozen of them, fearless and pushy, acting for all the world like a teen-aged street gang. They walked on and over me, perching on my head and jumping down into the cabin. After literally carrying them out I had to put the hatch screens on, thus further cutting down the ventilation reaching the steamy interior.

Their fishy droppings were everywhere. I'd no sooner sluice down the sails and the deck in the morning than the gang would return from a pre-dawn fishing trip and turn *Serenity* into a floating toilet bowl – no sense of occasion, or of being proper guests. Meanwhile, the sun was so hot I couldn't walk on deck in bare feet; and the green-grey droppings practically sizzled on the hot fibreglass. Even Irving, my little North Atlantic companion, had more class. It took two days before they took it into their heads to leave, and two more days to get the deck clean again.

Because of the heat and the boredom I swam almost every day. The pictures I took make life aboard look like a happy, sun-drenched frolic, yet the minutae were anything but. I had to subdivide my tasks and establish priorities to keep order on *Serenity*. Should I cut my toenails now or wait until tomorrow? Should I sew that torn pillowslip? Should I change the oil in the engine? A moment of big excitement was stepping on my glasses and the challenge of glueing them back together. I had plenty of time to practise with my sextant, but the only other benefit was that a bilge-soaked roll of toilet paper, my log, almanac, charts, tables, and bedding had all dried out in the heat. All were ready for another soaking as soon as the wind came up. Life had never been so basic.

I had had something of the same sense of waiting, waiting endlessly for something to happen, after I left Trizec. But even in this, my first solo business endeavour, I was not alone.

I gave birth to D.G. Philpott & Associates Limited in

January, 1973, with one of the country's largest legal firms, Blake Cassels & Graydon, as midwife. My wife and children acted as godparents by becoming minority shareholders.

The company was all fuelled up, with nowhere to go. I had ample working capital, but no projects. In the Yellow Pages I was listed as a developer, but my charter allowed me to do almost anything, including manufacturing, publishing, research, producing movies, and consulting. For more than twenty years I had been disciplined in the routines of office life. Other people's money had provided me with space, furniture, telephone, staff, and, above all, a secretary.

During those early months when I was in corporate diapers I chose not to run up any overhead costs whatsoever and worked out of my house in Oakville. Nothing could have been worse for my morale. I had a small office in the basement, equipped with a telephone and a typewriter, but I never felt that I was really in business. I did not leave the house at seven-thirty or eight o'clock in the morning, which, as anyone knows, is an absolute prerequisite. I typed my own letters: bush league.

Wanda understood that I was going through a confusing period and kept her distance during the business day; yet I was forever running into her by accident. A successful business-man has only superficial contact with his wife and family during business hours, and he certainly should never be expected to co-exist with the cleaning lady, who confronted me every Monday.

I shouldn't really complain, however, since I made money during those early months and set the wheels in motion for deals that galvanized into real projects in the years to come. But working out of an office in my house was decidedly Mickey Mouse.

In May, 1973, I received a call from George Hamann, the architect, who tipped me off that the Reichmann brothers of Olympia & York could use some help on what would become First Canadian Place. This seventy-two-storey office building was slated to have approximately half a million square feet of retail space at the lower levels, and the Reichmanns needed someone to give them a hand on the design and marketing of this huge facility.

Fresh from my success with Trizec's Scarborough Town Centre, I came to an agreement with this legendary family to provide Olympia & York with advice and consulting services for a comfortable fee and a furnished office in one of their buildings in downtown Toronto. I was back in the mainstream of the development industry, associated with two of the most aggressive and highly respected businessmen in North America, with a staff and office of my own. I located in the *Star* building at One Yonge Street, but I was later proud to see my company name on the directory board of First Canadian Place, nestled precociously among the country's most prestigious corporations and professional firms. It looked good and it felt right. I was happy.

I was particularly happy with my work and my relationship with the Reichmanns. At that time their holdings were limited to major commercial developments in southern Ontario, some manufacturing firms and industrial property, and one or two buildings in Montreal. I was to help guide the expansion of Olympia & York across Canada into the States. I negotiated the acquisition of properties, companies, and other interests all over North America.

Needless to say I was not the only outsider involved in these expansion efforts, but I was kept challenged and extremely busy for nearly eight years. I use the word "outsider" because decision-making was a family process, which, I gather, occurred on Sundays following Shabbat. Then the brothers and other members of the family would discuss the week's events and come to a consensus that, I understand, had to be unanimous.

The mystique of the Reichmanns remains to this day. One week I would orchestrate the introduction of Albert or Paul to a potential joint venture partner in Vancouver or Portland. The next week I might be in eastern Quebec, travelling with an unemployed rabbi, following up a real estate agent's claim that certain shopping centres were for sale. And as we wandered through small French-Canadian towns, I taught the rabbi real estate, and he taught me Jewish theology.

During the 1970s my company successfully entered the mortgage business and acquired positions in various pieces of commercial property across Canada. During this period I was also retained by small Ontario cities to advise them on urban redevelopment. I negotiated with developers for projects designed to reverse the trend towards central urban blight. In general, the people in these smaller cities had never done business with the powerful corporations I knew so well as either associate or adversary. Here I was dealing at the grass-roots level, and I found it a unique opportunity. I knew the language of land development, and knew it well. I negotiated on behalf of Sarnia, Brantford, North Bay, Tillsonburg, and others, opposite major developers with whom I had done business for many years. It was a new experience, one of the most rewarding of my career.

Over the years I developed many negotiating techniques, but one of my most effective was simple "staying power." I could work twenty-four hours at a stretch without food, rest, or relief. There was always some point in negotiations – usually approaching closing date – when a lengthy session was appropriate and I milked it for all it was worth. I applied negotiating pressure on lawyers, accountants, principals, municipal officials, and provincial representatives: we worked through lunch, dinner, and on into the wee hours; I was as fresh at two a.m. as my associates had been at ten the previous morning. I often wondered whether the process took talent or just a small stomach and a huge bladder.

I also knew the developers' strategies and tactics well, since I had invented many of them. Negotiating was a great and wonderful game. My clients profited, my company did well, and urban development sprang up all over southern Ontario. Life was good!

By 1978 my company, my corporate child, began to show signs of independence. As the company increased its earnings and influence, Joan Hammell, my assistant and right arm, was running the day-to-day operations. I was required only as an expert resource. Although potential conflicts of interest had forced me to drop my membership on the board of Trizec Corporation, I still had a good working relationship with the Reichmanns, and my cities were all doing well. I had to admit, however, that I had plateaued out.

I had had the thrill of giving birth to a company, of watching it grow and seeing it become self-sufficient. The adrenalin had surged, the heart had pounded, the sweat had flowed. Would it ever happen again?

By my early fifties I had experienced everything the conventional business world had to offer. I had helped create a multinational public corporation, in which I had power and prestige; I had been instrumental in the creation of major developments that received international acclaim. And, finally, I had proven that I could make it on my own. All my life I had tested my limits. Like an athlete, I pushed a bit harder for each contest. But at fifty years old I had run out of games to win and arenas in which to play them. Although I did not realize it at the time, I was searching for the ultimate contest: physical, emotional, and spiritual survival, alone against insuperable odds. The great adventure.

Although I gave my full attention and energies to current work I was careful not to accept any ongoing responsibilities. I was barely conscious of the major turn my life was taking. I was now financially independent; D.G. Philpott & Associates Limited could take care of me and my family for the rest of our days; and Joan could run it for me.

For the first time I was confronted with the rare, sought after, and terrifying possibility of not working for a living. One side of the brain relishes the security and potential leisure; the other comes to the depressing conclusion that this man is no longer needed. I was too young to enjoy a terminal vacation but too sated and tested to accept the same things from life for another twenty years.

Enter a blue ten-speed bicycle, some maps, and an itch to go to sea.

Nearly two hundred years ago Coleridge's Ancient Mariner mesmerized the wedding guest with his description of the Doldrums:

> Down dropt the breeze, the sails dropt down,
> 'Twas sad as sad could be;
> And we did speak only to break
> The silence of the sea!
>
> All in a hot and copper sky,
> The bloody Sun, at noon,
> Right up above the mast did stand,
> No bigger than the Moon.

Day after day, day after day,
We stuck, nor breath nor motion;
As idle as a painted ship
Upon a painted ocean.

By August 5, I was 7° 30' north, 49° 46' west, or about 420 nautical miles north-northeast of the mouth of the Amazon River. My lethargy was such that I hadn't made a journal entry for four days. I was fourteen days out of Antigua and nine of those had been spent cajoling us 220 miles south through the Doldrums. Yet I still tried to do some "sailing" to take whatever advantage I could of the intermittent winds.

It's quite possible that the lengendary curse of the Doldrums, which destroyed the souls of so many ancient mariners, might have been broken if there had been operas and orchestras at sea. Verdi, Puccini, Handel, and Brahms became essential to my life during those dead days of August.

The first ship I'd seen since leaving Antigua, the *Maasbee*, bound for Capetown, passed half a mile astern about 1650 hours, and I raised it on the radio. The skipper assured me that I'd soon be out of the Doldrums. He also told me that, two days earlier, the first hurricane of the season had passed a mere 240 miles north of our present position and was on its way from Barbados to the Caribbean. (My God! A few more days waiting in Antigua . . .) Wishing me bon voyage, *Maasbee* soon disappeared over the southern horizon.

On August 6, I recorded this radio newscast:

> *Hurricane Allen roared toward western Cuba and the Gulf of Mexico last night, leaving behind at least 68 dead and a swath of devastation stretching more than 1,000 miles across the Caribbean.*
>
> *The storm raked Jamaica with 100-mile-an-hour winds and torrential rain earlier in the day and skirted the Cayman Islands on its way north and west.*
>
> *Waves whipped by Allen dragged five people from their homes and drowned them in the sea at Port Maria on Jamaica's northern coast, according to published reports. In Kingston, a man was*

electrocuted by a powerline and two others died in
storm-related incidents.

The storm tore at the southern part of Hispaniola,
the island shared by Haiti and the Dominican
Republic, before crashing into Jamaica's northern
coast. Amateur radio operators reported up to 40 per
cent of the houses were destroyed near Les Cayes on
Haiti's southwestern coast.

Officials feared the toll would rise dramatically
with reports from isolated areas. The death count so
far: 8 in Jamaica, 41 in Haiti, 3 in the Dominican
Republic and 16 killed on Monday when Allen
slammed into the tiny eastern Caribbean island of St.
Lucia with 175 mph winds. In nearby Dominica, one
person was missing and feared dead.

The U.S. National Weather Service said the
hurricane, with sustained winds of 130 mph, was
expected to become stronger again after it moved
away from Jamaica on its way toward Cuba.

The storm, 350 nautical miles south of Florida,
was moving north-northwest toward the Gulf of
Mexico.

When I awoke the following morning, the *Maasbee*'s obser-
vation proved correct. I was, indeed, leaving the Doldrums.
The night before I had made a reckoning that I was close to the
northern rim of the southeast trades and, as though confirming my calculations, there had been a lively ripple on the
water. The squalls had come closer, one on another, and there
was an ineffable freshness to the air.

By 0930 hours on August 6, the breeze had freshened into a
force five. Little *Serenity* bowed to her partner, raised her
skirts, and danced across the waves, making five knots. Her
nine days in the Doldrums had been like having the flu; now,
with the agility that only small boats have, she became air-
borne off the crest of one wave before landing in the trough
and scampering up to the next. The movement inside the boat
was violent but welcome after days of sullen wallowing and
roasting in the tropical heat.

Zubin Mehta conducting the Israel Philharmonic Orchestra

in Mahler's Fourth Symphony was my soundtrack as we crossed into the southeast trades. The frantic violins, in the third movement, had been quieted by the horns, and the timpanist was reaching a crescendo, when I realized that I was on the homestretch: I was going to make it. Even with 4,000 miles to go, I knew that *Serenity* and I had the right stuff to take on the South Atlantic.

The flutes and violins took over from the percussion and the third movement ended. The fourth was about to begin.

Because I wanted to stay well clear of the South American coast, I was forced to sail close-hauled. Unfortunately, my preferred course was southeast, right into the eye of the wind. I had to tack south for a day or so, then come about on the starboard tack to a course almost due east; but always I was working myself toward my mid-Atlantic milepost.

I was aiming to round Arquo de Fernando de Noronha, a tiny island 350 miles off the hump of the Brazilian coast. From there I could swing to a more southerly direction and take maximum advantage of the prevailing winds. I was maintaining a steady speed of about five knots and was hoping to cross the equator on August 10, my fifty-third birthday; but by August 9, four days into the southeast trades, it was clear I wasn't going to make it.

The currents, the harmless-looking green arrows on the chart, had been against me and I had underestimated their effect. The difference between my sextant fix and my dead-reckoning position was often as much as thirty miles; a 1.5 knot current dead against me could take thirty-six miles a day off my forward progress.

Not meeting Neptune on my birthday was only a minor disappointment, and I revelled in the sailing conditions. The sun was shining almost all the time and there were fluffy, friendly clouds scattered about. The wind was constant force five, between nineteen and twenty knots, and *Serenity* was throwing out great plumes of spray from her bow. With her lee rail buried and a fringe of white froth fanning out for 200 feet astern, she was seducing me forever from the corporate boardroom.

I was paying a price, however, in bruises, bumps, abrasions, and stretched muscles. Below, the cabin tilted at an angle of

25°-30° and there was a fore-and-aft pitching as the boat went from crest to crest. As a result, I was almost weightless as the boat dropped, then I was slammed hard against a bulkhead as the boat landed in a trough. The cycle never ended, and I got relief only in sleep, where, curiously, the motion was soothing.

I was sleeping ten to twelve hours a night, broken by the obligatory on-deck checks for course and trim. For every motion on the boat, a sailor must make a counter motion; my muscles working all the time were letting me know about it. This is undoubtedly why an old insomniac like me slept the sleep of the just.

After days of drifting, I was now trying to make up time by taking advantage of *Serenity*'s ability to point, to sail up into the wind.

I spent as much as three or four hours a day taking sextant sights and doing the calculations. The stable conditions under which I learned navigation – fifteen feet or more above the water, on the solid ground of the Port Credit Yacht Club, looking south over Lake Ontario – were far different than those at sea. Now I was taking the sights from a deck that seemed alive beneath me, surrounded by eight- to twelve-foot waves superimposed on twenty-foot swells obliterating the horizon. I was learning to keep an ear cocked for the sound of the "big one," the wave that would break in a sheet of spray over the cockpit. Each time salt water landed on the sextant, I had to go below and carefully wipe off the mirrors, filters, and lenses with tissue. Back on deck, I was only six or seven feet above the surface, and I would often get readings that were way off. These maverick figures were culled after I compared the half-dozen results I collected from each round of sights. I would then average those remaining.

I always knew approximately where I was by dead reckoning, that is, using direction and distance from my last fix to establish a position. Over long distances, however, a DR position is unsatisfactory because of currents, leeway, and slight inaccuracies of compass and odometer. It is the sextant sight taken every few hours and followed by calculations using precise time that gives the sailor an accurate "fix" from which he can plot his course and DR positions. Pencilled notes, X's,

130

lines, and symbols eased slowly down the Atlantic chart, tracing my erratic route from Antigua. After each round of calculations I would make my entry, and the cat-scratches moved a fraction of an inch south and east.

I seemed able to cope with almost any navigation, mechanical, or sailing test, but there was one nagging problem that baffled me: salt. Salt was everywhere and into everything. Since it absorbs moisture from the air there was little aboard that wasn't clammy or slippery. The cabin sole was constantly wet from water splashing in through the companionway or tracked by me. Even when it seemed dry, the sole would become wet when night fell, as if by some perverse magic. When the temperature dropped, the condensing water vapour was absorbed by the salt, making for a slippery, dangerous footing. Moreover, my bedclothes and pyjamas were almost perpetually soggy, and I was forced to rinse them in my precious fresh water or rush up on deck to catch one of the infrequent rain squalls.

It was my twentieth day out of Antigua. The sailing had been so exhilarating and time-consuming since the Doldrums that I'd read only one of the two dozen books I had brought along; I'd expected to finish a book every three or four days. I also realized that I'd been at sea longer than any vacation I'd ever taken from business, and as long as I'd spent cycling to Florida. I was breaking patterns, habits, and routines.

But disaster had struck, too. Of my stock of four rolls of toilet paper, three fell into the bilge! Until I established that they could be dried out and revived, strict rationing was imposed.

CHAPTER TEN

O N AUGUST 16, I SLEPT MY WAY ACROSS THE EQUATOR IN THE MIDDLE OF THE NIGHT ABOUT 5° farther west than I had anticipated – those currents again. I toyed with the idea of performing some appropriate heathen rite of submission to Neptune the next morning but rejected it as too frivolous for a boat of *Serenity*'s heroic ilk. Such antics work well on cruise liners and large vessels, but their main requirement was an audience; I was reasonably sure Neptune would understand. The following morning I played Wagner's overtures to "Tannhäuser" and "The Flying Dutchman" to celebrate my passage into the Southern Hemisphere.

Day after day, sailing conditions had been beautiful. There were rough periods, but by now I hardly noticed them. I hadn't had any major equipment failures, and the problems so far were trivial and annoying rather than life-threatening: there was a small tear in the sail from chafing on the rigging; all my ball-point pens had run dry so I had to write the log in pencil; the matches were so damp I had to ignite them on the pilot light of the water heater; one deck winch was jammed; and a sail runner had come off. Only this last item was more significant than I realized.

The night before crossing the equator I had taken my steaming mug of Ovaltine topside to gaze at the most beautiful sky I've ever seen. The moon was new enough that, while it drew a path across the rolling water, it didn't illuminate the sky; and the stars stood out against a background of deep, black velvet. The air was pleasantly cool. This was the overture to Act II, in which *Serenity* and I would have to draw on all of our reserves. The ocean here was relatively gentle, and making a mistake in these waters was seldom serious; but the heavy seas and gale conditions in the great Southern Ocean would be unforgiving and an error could be fatal.

Serenity's electrical system was set up to ensure that the diesel engine could generate power. One battery was always switched out and held as a spare after the engine had charged up the system. It would then be available to turn over the starting motor should the other three batteries run down. I carefully rationed my electricity because the tank held just enough fuel to generate limited power for ninety days and allow me to manoeuvre through Capetown harbour.

The day after I crossed the equator, I fired up the Volvo and charged the batteries for three hours. Five days later all four batteries were dead. I had committed the cardinal sin of neglecting to switch out the spare unit. The engine could not be started; I could no longer generate power.

I had not only a *Volvo Users' Handbook*, but a diesel repair manual as well. I followed the instructions meticulously, but try as I might the engine remained stubbornly silent, refusing all my attempts to start it manually. I would try many times during the days to come, but the engine had given up.

Music was my only real loss. Without electricity, Tchaikovsky, Rachmaninoff, and Vivaldi were gone, taking their symphonies, concertos, and sonatas with them. Not till Capetown would I hear von Karajan, Gould, or Domingo. They were all important members of my crew and would be sorely missed.

> *AUGUST 21:*
>
> *1240 HOURS:*
>
> *This is literally a turning point in the journey. I've just taken Fernando de Noronha 75 miles off to the starboard. This, of course, is of absolutely no consequence to anybody but myself; it does, however, put me in a position wherein I can govern my own direction without having to concern myself with perverse winds and currents. . . . This point has been my goal for about a week now. I've travelled 2,170 nautical miles from Antigua as the crow flies but had to pass through 2,900 miles of water. . . . Every inch of the 2,900 miles was beating into the wind close-hauled, and the currents were taking me one step back for every three forward.*
>
> *Ten minutes ago, I payed out the mainsheet and*

am now on a broad reach, heading on a course of 185°, and within the next couple of hundred miles I should have currents with me instead of forcing me back. As soon as I eased the sail and set the new course, Serenity knew exactly how to play the game! She sped up from 5 to 6 knots and the movement of the boat is much easier.

Until this point I had been unable to follow the sailing routes as described in Ocean Passages of the World published by the British Admiralty. The passage I've just completed is shown as a course for vessels travelling north up the coast of South America and heading towards southern ports in the United States. I knew when I left Antigua I would be travelling "upstream" so to speak, against this route.

Finally I am in that position which has, for centuries, been the decision point for southbound sailing vessels that intend, after crossing the equator, to head along the coast of South America or swing around over to the Cape of Good Hope and on to Australia. I intend to follow this latter course. It has been proven over many years and was the route of the Clipper ships in the middle of the last century. It will lead me south to a point opposite Rio de Janeiro, from where I will start to work my way east and south until I am on the same latitude as Capetown.

During the whole distance, I hope to be on a broad reach, that is to say with the wind on the beam, which is the optimum relationship to the wind for any sailing craft, especially Serenity.

The U.S. pilot chart of the South Atlantic confirms the admiralty sailing instructions . . . so I'm now in the wake of the Clipper ships, and Serenity is already pushing over 6 knots in her attempt to beat the time of her forebears.

I spent a great deal of time in the cockpit, a slightly older caricature of those bronzed gods who inhabit beer commercials. I was bronzed, but no longer bare-chested. The air had enough of a nip in it, even in the sunny periods, to require a

134

shirt; and when the wind was up and the boat was racing along, I needed my yellow nylon shell as a windbreak.

I was keeping a very close eye on the head of the mast. A weakness had begun to develop in the sail when a sail runner tore loose. I had made the necessary repairs but two more runners were showing signs of fatigue. I had shortened sail one tuck and suspect this was putting an added strain (although well within reasonable limits) on the sail track, runners, and fabric. That one runner showing weakness had made me suspicious, and the next morning, when I found four more runners broken loose, it confirmed my fears that my sail was faulty. The luff had been made without a bolt rope or layering of fabric adequate to give the grommets firm purchase. Two of the grommets were nowhere to be found, flung violently away by the whipping of the sail, itself flapping awkwardly without the runners.

I spent four hours trying to repair the damage with my sail-mending kit and lecturing myself for not minutely examining the new sail before the mast was stepped in Antigua.

By August 26, five days past Fernando de Noronha, I had covered as much distance – some 690 miles – as I had the previous ten days, bucking against wind and current. A steady force five east wind had built up a very heavy sea; green water broke over the bow and soaked everything that was uncovered.

On the twenty-seventh, I awoke to a calm morning and rushed to dry things out. I even used some of my precious fresh water to do a complete wash and to get the salt out of my bed clothes and underclothing. In the process I dropped an open bottle of shampoo in the cockpit and created an impromptu slapstick comedy routine, with suds billowing everywhere. I must have pumped a hundred gallons of sea water into the cockpit to flush it all away.

Without electricity, I shut off the odometer and speedometer, leaving me to estimate my distances and speed for dead-reckoning. This was not as serious as it sounds, as I was taking sights at least once a day and my location was known at all times. If I wasn't able to estimate speed and distance without instruments by now I never would be. However, the loss of power did force me to schedule my life to the sun. I timed all my activities to end at dusk, about 5:30; after that I'd just lie

135

on my bunk in the dark waiting to fall asleep, listening to the wind and the rushing cadence of the bow wave.

A few months earlier, the very thought of being inactive for longer than thirty seconds was abhorrent; it offended my drive and ambition. But now I found this enforced inactivity was good for me. Very few of us have real solitude. There was absolutely no possibility of interruption, short of a sailing emergency: no neighbours, no deals, no telephone, no radio, no TV, no diversions, and, surprisingly, no worries. For the first time in years, I began to think about myself as a person, unrelated to career, business, or family. Who I was and from where I'd come.

I also thought about my brother Peter and *Pristis*, our first little boat. We bought the heavy, mahogany hull in very bad condition in 1941 for sixty dollars, but christened it after a far more glamorous vessel I'd read about in Greek mythology. Peter and I had hacked about in a cedar-strip Peterborough canoe with a primitive mast and lateen rig; but this little Bermuda-rigged sloop was a true sailing dinghy. We had to do so much work to make it seaworthy that we learned a good deal about boat building. From *Pristis*, too, I must have contracted the sailing disease that, in spite of periods of remission, had proved incurable.

We'd come to sailing naturally when our family summered on the Toronto Islands. In those days it was still fashionable, decades before it became controversial; and summering on the islands was not unusual for the upper-middle-class people who were our Rosedale neighbours.

When we were forced to live there year-round, coping with the icy winds off the lake in mid-January, it was a far different world. Still, for teen-aged boys, the islands were glorious, particularly in those warm breezy summer days during and just after World War II. From our narrow, adolescent perspective, with pocket money from summer jobs and all the sailing we could handle, we were riding high. There also seemed to be no scarcity of girls eager to become our captives out on the bay. We should have felt oppressed and threatened by the war and the financial straits of our family, I suppose, but I recall only that life was pleasant, exciting, and less complicated than it had ever been since.

136

When I awoke the next morning, I was overpowered by the conviction that I must push on past Capetown to Melbourne and Cape Horn. I became gripped by a compulsion bordering on religious zeal. It was at that moment that my earlier decision to circumnavigate was galvanized into an irrevocable commitment.

All along I had been temporizing, partly out of a fear of failure but more because I had wanted to avoid any disciplines. The whole trip was a radical departure from my normal way of doing things, and I was shying away from the kind of decision-making that had been such an integral part of my life before *Serenity*. Analysis, priority, estimates, risk – the development business lived off such considerations, with a generous helping of luck. The luck that had remained with me on land would, I was sure, stay with me at sea.

Until that morning I had tried to let events unfold as something of a surprise, although I had been far-sighted enough to get charts and even an Australian visa, and to travel in a well-prepared vessel that could carry me all the way. The idea of circumnavigation had been there since Antigua, but I knew, way back in the far reaches of my head bone, that I could always reconsider and terminate the venture in Capetown. Now nothing was going to stop me from realizing my ambition, a single-handed voyage around the world. My goal would be the attempt.

As I shaved, which I did daily, a face I hadn't seen before stared back at me. That bleached-out haystack of hair was there; but there was a softer look; lines seemed to be disappearing from around my mouth, and there was a bright glint in my eyes. A sceptic might say this was all due to fresh air and twelve hours' sleep a night, which might be true in part. But I'd begun to lose that manic sense of urgency, and I was all the better for it.

> *AUGUST 23:*
>
> *0930 HOURS:*
>
> *Yesterday I entered what I presumed to be the horse latitudes. This is an area of ocean between the trade winds and the prevailing westerlies that is fraught with uncertain weather and little wind. Legend has it that voyagers of long ago, who happened to be*

137

*carrying horses on board, threw the creatures
overboard at this point because the animals were
consuming water much needed by the crew and
passengers.*

*I would like to add some new trivia to ocean lore.
The sea is not to be feared solely as a destroyer of
ships, an eroder of land, a power beyond man's
control. I am quite certain that the ocean is primarily
dedicated to one thing only: the destruction of
zippers. Every jacket, pair of trousers, garment bag
and other zippered items I have on board have been
rendered completely inoperative by the ravages of the
sea. I sincerely hope it is warm enough in Capetown
to disembark in a bathing suit and T-shirt because
the necessary hardware on my slacks has all but
disappeared.*

At dawn on August 29, I was double-reefed and got hammered
by a force eight gale. Most of the runners and their grommets
were ripped from the fabric, leaving me wallowing at the
mercy of the storm. For more than an hour I struggled in the
howling wind and spray, trying to transfer the main halyard
from the now crippled mainsail to the smaller stormsail that
had been hanked to the mast on the duplicate track.

After four days of spasmodic but uneventful sailing in the
horse latitudes, I had entered the prevailing westerlies with
their monstrous swells, which I estimated to be forty feet high
and about a quarter of a mile apart. It was almost impossible,
under these conditions, to work quickly, tied to the boat by
my safety harness and hanging on to the mast with one hand.
The wind literally snatched the lines from me time and again.

I finally got my small sail flying but found it incapable of
holding *Serenity* close-hauled into the wind. My intended
course was approximately due south and I was bucking a gale
from the southwest. I was forced to take the wind on the starboard beam, which sent *Serenity* scudding down the great
waves in a southeast direction at a speed of five to six knots.

I was pointed straight at Capetown; but this course was
going to take me into an area of wind that would shift to the
east at this latitude, so I had to get myself farther south before

I made any progress towards Africa. It was essential that I raise the large sail as soon as possible. I jammed the huge bundle of wet dacron through the companionway into the cold, damp cabin below and started on the repairs.

By noon the wind was down to force six and holding; I would have liked to work *Serenity* up into a more southerly course but high winds, smashing waves, and the small sail were too much for her – she would not answer her helm.

It was about 1420 hours when the topping-lift parted from the end of the wishbone and flew to the top of the mast. Although not serious, it was an irritation and, in such weather, the very devil to retrieve. I ignored it, hoping a slight shift of wind would allow me to come about on the port tack and reduce the beating the boat was taking. I turned the wheel. Suddenly, the wave pattern changed. *Serenity* careened down into a trough, momentarily out of control. The hundred-pound, thirty-foot-long aluminum wishbone hurtled across the cockpit and smashed into the side of my head.

I had forgotten that, without the topping-lift, the stormsail and wishbone hung much lower than with the main. Normally it would have cleared me by a foot or more, but instead it drove into my skull. I will never know how long I was out. Water was splashing off my face as I came around, laid out face up in the bottom of the cockpit. I couldn't move. The storm-sail flogged angrily above me, fastened loosely to the wildly swinging wishbone. The mast was whipping like a fly rod.

I tried to sit up to escape the cascades of water that dumped on me from all directions, but my arms would not respond. Gingerly lifting my head, I discovered that the safety harness and life line had trussed me up, pinning both elbows to my sides. I lay still for a minute or more, allowing life to come back into focus. I methodically removed the tangle of rope that held me and sat up.

I was an omelet!

All I could think of, through a spluttering giggle, was that I was a broken egg on a white plate, covered with catsup. I looked at myself. The bright yellow storm-suit was stark against the white deck. Blood, from diluted pink to dark red, was everywhere.

Panic gripped me. I was blind on the left side. Hoping that

my parka was obscuring my vision, I tugged at it, to no effect. Then my fingers felt warm, sticky flesh.

The boom had carved a two-inch square flap of skin off my forehead, and it dangled over my eye like a grizzly pirate's patch. As I struggled to my feet, I spat out a piece of tooth. I dropped down to the bloody puddle in the cockpit, fishing about trying to retrieve it, with the insane thought that it might be put back in when I got to Capetown.

The boat had come about on its own. Somehow I secured the main-sheet, adjusted the self-steering gear, and groggily clambered down into the head for a look in the mirror. It was disgusting! Blood streamed down the side of my face, and everywhere I touched it smeared, fouling and staining the bulkheads.

All my moves were slow and calculated. I remained remarkably cool. I knew that I probably had a concussion and that my head gash required sutures. Although I had a well-stocked first-aid kit, it was beyond my limited medical abilities. I blotted the blood up with towelling and toilet tissue, avoiding the pink bone beneath. I gently lifted the offending flap and fastened the two parts of my forehead together as best as I could with three band-aids.

My head was beginning to throb and swell; it felt as if it were stuffed with cotton. I lay down on my bunk and drifted off, confident that the boat would continue at four knots on the set course.

I wakened from my half sleep about 1700 hours, just before dusk, and looked through the skylight. In numbed disbelief, I watched the stormsail. The top of the sail was flying free of the mast; the runners were gone, and the wind was wrenching the remaining grommets from the fabric – exactly like the mainsail. I had no choice but to put on the blood-stained foul-weather gear once again and climb on deck – keeping a wary eye on that wishbone – to take down the disabled stormsail, letting *Serenity* lie-a-hull. I returned to my bunk exhausted and slept.

I spent the next day sewing grommets into the main. I cannibalized the stormsail for sail runners and other hardware, reasoning that if I could just bend the repaired mainsail onto the mast, I'd make it.

My earlier plan had been to work on the large sail while the

140

stormsail carried me on into calmer weather; but I was now forced to choose one sail or the other. The small tri-sail had proven incapable of holding *Serenity* on an up-wind tack and was severely damaged, so I opted for the main. I worked on into the night by the light of an oil lamp; after a short sleep, I completed the repair work by noon the following day. I had to cut new holes for grommets and reinforce them with yards of nylon thread, locking each eyelet well back into the fabric so that it would not tear loose again.

One side of my face was blue and puffy. I looked haggard and still felt groggy; I realized afterwards I was probably suffering not only from concussion but shock. The wound on my forehead looked clean, and I expected that I'd have a helluva scar.

After five hours' work on a gyrating deck, I got the renovated mainsail up from below onto the mast and working. I'd seen better looking canvas, but it set well and *Serenity* was barrelling along at about six and a half knots in roughly the direction I wanted to go. Without sun, I had only a vague notion where I was, and it was still too rough to get an accurate sight.

I lay down on my bunk, fully clothed, and slept.

Over the next few days, the weather was relatively co-operative, the barometer holding level or rising slightly, and most of my time was spent trimming sails, adjusting George, and coercing *Serenity* back to order, working my way to a more southerly course. The sail repair was not holding very well, and I worked below on the stormsail preparing for the day I would have to use it again. Still, the boat was handling remarkably well, considering I was forced to compromise speed and direction in order to minimize the pressure of the wind on the sail. The weather continued to co-operate and our speed ranged from four to seven knots.

Most of my days at sea included some attention to minor breakdowns and mishaps; a routine watch was made up of a hundred tiny chores and diversions. September 2 was certainly not typical, but seemed to prove the old adage that misfortunes come in bunches:

> *I got up at 0600 hours and put on some coffee to heat. But a glance out of the companionway showed*

that clouds were coming in, and I set aside mug and book and took the morning sight while I could still see the sun. Result: cold coffee.

I made some hot porridge; but just as it was ready, the clew parted from the wishbone, leaving the sail flailing in the wind . . . two hours of emergency repairs. Result: dried-up porridge.

I remade the cereal and the coffee, and luxuriated for twenty minutes in the warmth and comfort, cradling the heavy stoneware cup and writing a log entry. My reverie was ended by a nagging, groaning noise from up forward, a reminder of a problem that had been bothering me for some time. The mast sat in a step of reinforced fibreglass, which apparently had been stretched or had become worn from the movement of the aluminum mast. I fashioned some hardwood wedges with my handsaw and pounded them into place around the base.

The job had to be hurried, however, because noon was upon me and I had to be on deck for more sights, to do my calculations, and to plot a revised course from the fix and check it against the pilot chart.

After all was done and I had written up the log entry, I thought I'd have time for some lunch; but the wishbone parted from the mainsheet and the whole assembly swung around forward of the bow. The wind was gathering strength and the spray was raking the deck. Once topside I found that the block had broken at the wishbone. The job was to get the boat facing into the wind so that I could effect a repair. Without the engine, it took an hour to bring the boat about by pure muscle power; there were blood stains on the sail from my raw hands to record the effort.

An hour later I'd repaired the block and gone below, chilled and dispirited, only to find that the tossing about of the boat had loosened the wedges around the mast step and the job had to be done again.

142

*All this plus the routine sailing chores – checking
of gear, cleaning up and drying wet clothes and
bedding, ablutions, and general housekeeping, all
within the time disciplines of 6 a.m. to 6 p.m. when
the light faded with an evening meal yet to prepare.
No long-distance sailor is ever at a loss to explain
what he does all day.*

My noon fix on September 4 showed that I was officially in the
Southern Ocean, having crossed the Tropic of Capricorn at
about 2015 hours the previous evening. I was in the last throes
of the southern winter, and each evening was a little bit
cooler. When I left Antigua, I was sleeping under a light sheet;
now I had a wool blanket and pyjamas.

Despite the limited drawing power of my sail, I had my best
day on September 3. I covered 146 miles with a steady,
friendly wind on the port quarter; indeed, I'd been on a broad
reach for days with winds ranging from force three to force five
(8 to 24 miles per hour). Besides making excellent time, I was
putting the least possible strain on my sails. Fortunately, I'd
been able to keep full sail for four straight days, as reefing put
excessive strain on the vulnerable grommets.

By the morning of September 5, however, I woke to a wind
climbing upward of force seven and swinging aft towards the
starboard quarter. The change in wind was piling up confused
waves of eight to twelve feet, and slate-grey clouds were closing in from the horizon, settling into an unbroken ceiling
about 100 feet above the water. The rain started, light at first,
then increasing in force until each drop was like a steel pellet
smacking against my face. The sea was black, cross-hatched
with whitecaps and streaks of foam. I felt the same chill run
up my spine that I experienced during the first ferocious ocean
gale between Halifax and Bermuda. I knew I was in for a lot of
this kind of weather now that I was in the Southern Ocean,
and even more as I approached the Roaring 40s, that ring of
wind around the globe just south of the major land masses –
restless, fierce, and justifiably the stuff of legends.

Serenity tended to be at her best in such conditions, provided that her equipment or master didn't let her down.
Averaging about eight knots, we surged to ten and a half for

extended periods, an "impossible" speed for a boat this size, made possible by surfing just forward of the breaking crest of the great combers that came rolling up from behind.

More of the runners had parted from the sail, but I expected we could hold out as long as the breeze stayed below force seven and I could hold the wind on the stern. If I was forced to reach or take a tuck in the sail I knew the remaining runners would go.

By first light next morning, after a sleepless night punctuated by near jibes that required me to go up on deck in the driving rain to alter course and prevent her from broaching, I estimated we'd covered 100 miles. But the wind was building to a full gale and I reluctantly had to reef. In the process, as expected, the upper sail runners tore out like an opening zipper because of the added strain reefing put on the top third of the sail.

I'd resigned myself to entering Capetown with the sail attached at only the tack, the head, and the clew, and there was no choice but to go with the force of the storm. It meant we were moving along at about six or seven knots with the wind behind us, slightly east of the course I wanted; but I dared change nothing until the sea settled down.

On September 7, almost from the moment I woke, the barometer began a slide that continued all day. A near-gale developed: seas were fourteen to sixteen feet, but the sun came out. It did nothing to dispel the cold, but it spread a warm patina over the angry water. I was feeling more confident, making good speed, on a very broad reach that allowed me to carry a lot of sail. This was making a virtue out of necessity because I was certain if I reefed again, the necessary slackening of the halyard would put too much strain on the unsupported sail and it would probably blow.

We were now approaching a full gale, but reefing was out of the question. *Serenity* seemed to relish the following wind and showed few signs of strain. The increasing violence of the sea, however, caused the wishbone to rise, emptying and refilling the sail with explosive force.

I brought the boat around onto a starboard tack to move in a more southerly direction; I hoped that, with the waves piling in on the starboard quarter, *Serenity* would be less inclined to lurch and bounce. With the wishbone out on the port side held down with a vang, and the sail taut and shivering, George worked without complaint. I liked what I saw. With about three hours of sunshine left I went below.

Suddenly she broached.

CHAPTER ELEVEN

"*T*RISTAN *DA CUNHA POKES THIRTY-SEVEN SQUARE MILES OF VOLCANIC ROCK OUT OF THE SOUTH AT-* lantic. An eruption in 1961 forced the two hundred and sixty four inhabitants to flee. After eighteen months' exile in England, some two hundred chose to return. Latitude 37° 03 minutes south 12° 18 minutes west."

Hardly a gripping narrative and certainly not bursting with fascinating information; but it was all I'd been able to glean from the *National Geographic Atlas* and my *Bowditch*. This is not material for the cocktail circuit, but it was vital to me: Tristan da Cunha was the nearest land, and I intended to reach it.

For the three days following the loss of my halyard, I'd been blown south at about thirty to forty miles per day. At the same time I was being driven northeast at about seventeen to twenty miles a day by the Falkland current, which originates in the frigid waters south of Cape Horn. Theoretically, the combined forces of wind and current should move me south-easterly at about fifteen miles a day. This hypothesis put me three or four weeks from my goal.

George had been put back to work. Repairing self-steering gear required hours of drilling through the aluminum castings. In order to free both hands to manipulate the drill I had to lash myself, in a contorted kneeling position, to the tiny lumpy surface of the gyrating after-deck. A generous lacing of fibreglass and epoxy contributed to George's health and well-being, but unfortunately, without power or sail, the plywood vane flopped about impotently, surrendering my course to the whims of the elements.

Somehow, I had to raise a sail. With a sail I could get more speed; with speed I could steer.

The top half of my useless main writhed violently and agonizingly from the head of the mast. If the gale would slacken, for just a moment, the dacron remnant could drop close enough to the deck for me to reach it and unwind the tangled mess of fabric and rope above. I constructed a twenty-four-foot long pole with a hook at one end to extend my reach in case an unlikely opportunity presented itself. If I could just drag either halyard down from the head of the mast I could raise my small stormsail and *Serenity* would come back to life.

My present situation was, in part, the consequence of my failing to examine the new sail when it was delivered to me in Antigua. I had blown out many sails in a lifetime on the water, but never had I had one part at the luff, carrying the halyard to the head of the mast. A respectable, well-behaved sail will burst in many different ways, but in my experience, a tattered but unbroken portion of the sail always remained clinging to the mast, allowing the remains to be drawn down to the deck along with the halyard. The damaged sail would then be set aside, a new one hanked to the sail track, hauled up the mast, and the boat would be underway again in a matter of minutes.

After failing to draw the main halyard down to the deck, I had attempted to use my second halyard, but it had been fouled at the masthead by number one and was unusable. Without so much as a hope of success, I'd attempted to scale the mast to attach a temporary block about ten feet above the deck. I had hoped to feed a line through the block to hoist the small stormsail. With my safety harness clipped to a loop around the mast I would start shinnying up the spar, only to find myself forced to clench the aluminum with both arms and legs. My climbing pole described a 160° arc, carrying me, in a terrifying trajectory, from a horizontal position on the starboard side over to the black water below, on the port.

I had enough fuel to take me about half the way to Tristan da Cunha but my erstwhile faithful engine refused to start. I cajoled and pleaded, checking filters, releasing and reinstating compression, and continuously spinning the heavy flywheel. I would give up only to try and try again as the days wore on, searching the handbooks for the secret. The engine would not only give me the lifesaving propulsion I needed, but it could also provide electrical power to replace the dwindling energy of the dry cells I was using occasionally to operate my VHF radio. Visually, I was a pinprick on the ocean surface; but a radio, giving out Mayday signals, would expand my discovery radius to about sixty miles, thus immeasurably increasing my chances of being rescued. And rescue was fast appearing to be my only way out.

The odds were certainly not on my being able to pick up a volcanic pimple on the surface of a 4,000-mile-wide ocean without sail or power; however, I did everything I could to maintain a generally southeast course. I pictured myself raising the island on the horizon, inflating my Avon dinghy, and rowing ashore through the ocean swells and cresting waves to be received with awe and wonderment by two hundred Tristan da Cunhaians – fat chance!

Murphy's Law seemed to be applied with dispiriting frequency. Not content with leaving me a disabled hulk, the fates now extinguished my battery strobe light, the one beacon I'd be counting on to make *Serenity* visible at night to the lookout on a passing ship. About four p.m. on September 13, I tried to switch on the flashing strobe; I would hoist it, as high as possible, on the topping lift as I had done every night since being disabled. The light was dead. I had five spare batteries, but batteries weren't the problem; it was the lamp, and the spare had been broken already. Now I was truly invisible after dark. All I could do was get up every couple of hours and scan the horizon in the hope of seeing a vessel and attracting attention with flares.

By Sunday, September 14, the gale had continued for five days and four nights, keeping me a virtual prisoner below decks as the wind drove me inexorably south. I had now completely given up any thought of raising Tristan da Cunha, as I could not hold a course. I'd streamed out more drogues from the port quarter and was towing the lower remnant of the mainsail to slow me down. The slower I moved, the longer I would stay within the shipping lanes and the possibility of rescue.

My oilskins provided little protection from the cascades of water. Most of the time the great mountains had been met by a glowering low ceiling of clouds that squeezed out vicious showers. I had become used to the corkscrewing motion, but

148

never to the unpredictable, occasional cresting of a wave that wrenched *Serenity* over on her beam with the mast just touching the water.

Below, everything was wet. Spray would sneak past me as the hatch was opened or the sea would find its way in through a briefly opened porthole. The gigantic waves that travel at right angles to the great ocean swells produced a particularly violent motion onboard *Serenity*; and the constant spilling of cooking water kept the cabin sole awash.

Sleep was next to impossible. With the bunks oriented bow to stern there was a tendency for my skin to stay put on the damp sheets while my inner being rolled around inside – a peculiar and uncomfortable sensation. On the third night I got the bright idea of setting up a bunk running across the width of the cabin. As the boat rolled, my head would drop four or five feet below my feet; a few seconds later, my extremities would exchange position, the cycle repeating itself throughout the night. Sickening as this sounds, it was the better alternative and I could sleep soundly.

The one thing that was difficult to deal with was the noise. When undersail, there was little sound but the hiss of the wake, the gurgle of water rippling past the hull, and the occasional sneeze as the bow smashed into a wave. Sitting in the ocean with no sails to steady the motion and no forward progress, every movement had a characteristic and unpleasant sound. The contents of drawers and lockers shifted from side to side in sympathy with the boat's motion; the food lockers seemed always to nominate one can or jar to roll about, no matter how carefully I stowed things. The mast, no longer held taut by a sail, flailed about like a northern sapling, rattling, groaning, and even screaming. And from the outside, the sea set up a constant, irregular pounding. I tried to cheer myself up by writing in my journal: "There is one nice thing about a gale at sea; it ends. One morning I am going to wake up to a blue sky, a gentle swell, and blessed silence."

But not yet. By 1500 hours on September 14 I was trying to make order out of the below-deck chaos. *Serenity* had been knocked down: the waves picked the boat up and laid it over on its side, plunging the mast underwater. That everything comes tumbling from its proper place is a minor irritation; the main problem is that everything becomes soaking wet, for the knock-down brings up or down all the bilge water. I sponged down the walls, ceilings, and upholstery; then I tried to rinse out my hair. I'd been drinking a cup of coffee when the explosion occurred, and now I was wearing it. The only small mercy was that we hadn't gone all the way and capsized. After some trouble, I found one of my three pairs of reading glasses, broken yet again, this time beyond repair.

It wasn't until September 16 that the gale ended its nine-day tirade. I woke that morning to blue sky, a heavily rolling sea – and sun. I bustled about washing my pillowslip and underwear, with at least an even chance of having them dry before the weather deteriorated again. The night before had been the coldest to date; I'd slept with a flannelette sheet and a wool blanket and, as the night wore on, I grabbed every article of clothing I could find and piled it over me, but with little effect. I capped the cabin ventilators in the hope that this would allow me to hold onto a little of the heat I generated with short bursts from the propane stove.

After hanging out my wash, I inspected the storm damage. Tension on at least one line had been so powerful that a pad eye had been ripped from its base. My large ensign, the Canadian flag, had been flying upside down, the international distress signal. Now it was little more than red and white ribbons. I replaced it.

While the storm forced me to be idle, I'd had time to give the matter of rescue a great deal of thought, or rather, fantasy. As I daydreamed, the rescue vessel took shape with an eerie clarity. It would be a white, shiny cruise ship with, of course, an English-speaking crew. In my journal I detailed my fancied rescue:

> It will first appear on the horizon as a white super-structure, slowly rising to show a long, sleek hull. On seeing my first orange distress smoke signal, it will turn in my direction and round up smartly on the weather side to keep me in the lee of the waves. I will be completely ready to abandon Serenity.
>
> Excited passengers will be clustered on all decks looking down at the tiny boat riding bravely on the waves below. The captain will ask me, through a

loud hailer, what is it that I need? I will respond,
without a loud hailer, that I very much regret that I
will have to abandon Serenity unless he can give me
a tow. With apologies he will state that, because of
his speed, he is unable to give me a tow but would
be pleased to take me onboard and notify the
authorities as to my location. I accept.

Four or five sailors lower lines so I can attach my
luggage and have it hauled onboard. A ladder is
dropped for me by the first officer. When I arrive on
deck I'm surrounded by dozens of chattering
passengers, thrilled at being part of a rescue at sea.

Briefly, almost casually, I give the captain an
account of the circumstances that disabled my
vessel. He will congratulate me on my seamanship
and express his condolences. He will ask me how I
managed to survive the past weeks of gales and high
seas; and I, with a shrug, will say, "It is nothing for
we men who go to sea."

Hot baths, slavish and attentive service, delicious
sleep, delicious food, and even more delicious coffee.
I'm assigned a white-jacketed servant, who washes
my T-shirt, windbreaker, and socks, presses my
slacks, and cleans my Adidas.

Before lunch at the captain's table I'm asked, as an
honour, to take the noon sight: I produce a perfect
set of figures. After an afternoon and evening
indifferently fending off awestruck, adoring females,
whose jealous husbands cower in the far reaches of
the main saloon, I retire to the owner's cabin, which
has been put at my disposal. Everyone stares at the
man cast up by the sea, blond, tanned, irresistible,
and above all, envied.

My bed has been turned down, Pierre Cardin
pyjamas are tastefully laid out beside a silk dressing
gown, and soft leather slippers are on the floor. Fresh
fruit and chocolate mints are on the dresser beside a
bucket of chilled wine. Sleep comes easily.

I didn't allow myself to dwell on less savoury scenarios –
this was my fantasy, after all, not my nightmare – such as the

Uruguayan smuggler who would strip my boat and leave me dead; the government vessel that refused to give aid because there's nothing in the book to cover the situation; or maybe some grimy oil freighter headed for Montevideo. None of that bore thinking about; besides, the fantasy filled the time. When the weather was sunny enough I sat in the cockpit, bundled against the wind, scanning the horizon for my ship.

Although the gale was over, the air had a bite and the seas remained high, but I could lie out in the cockpit in a ski jacket and be comfortable. The violent motion of the boat was preventing me from getting decent sights. I got three or four that, coupled with two different systems of calculations and educated estimates, indicated that I was about 31° south and 17° west. I abandoned these figures as having little or no validity because of the inaccuracy of my measurements. Unless the sea calmed down and the deck steadied, as it had been under sail, I was not going to be able to locate myself within 100 miles of my actual position. All hope of raising Tristan da Cunha was gone. Even if I was on course, which I wasn't, I could easily pass it in the night without ever knowing.

My one comfort was that I was close to the main shipping route between Rio de Janeiro and Capetown, and a couple hundred miles north of the Montevideo course, the most southerly of all ocean routes shown on my chart.

I was frankly amazed at the pounding *Serenity* was taking. She had faced up to weather into which much larger vessels would not venture, and she lay-a-hull, as she was now doing, without sustaining any apparent damage. The drogues that I had been streaming from the stern seemed to have had a beneficial effect, but I was not really certain. They were originally fixed to reduce my speed and keep the boat's stern to the waves in order to lessen my southerly progress and the rolling motion. There was a danger, however, that the drogues could slow the boat so much that a wave could break over the stern and smash through into the cabin. With that ominous possibility in mind, I'd been up on the deck during the previous night's gale, altering the drogues so that they streamed off the starboard quarter; *Serenity* was now dividing the waves between the beam and stern. Considering the enormous grey mountains moving towards us and the number of breaking waves, I thought the system seemed to be working. The motion down below was not as bad as during most of the last storm.

After almost sixty days of solitude I'd had lots of time for a heart-to-heart with myself, to isolate my goals and aspirations. My journal had become my companion. I talked to my cassette recorder as though it were a confidant. My thoughts of a given moment were entered in the journal without much retrospection and, of course, no knowledge of what the future held.

SEPTEMBER 13:

0730 HOURS:

Last night at 2000 hours we got hit with another gale that came in like an explosion, before it had a chance to build up a sea. I was able to "nail everything down" anticipating the worst. I think the savage, unrelenting violent motion of the boat was the most powerful I've experienced.

The storm died about 0200 this morning, as quickly as it had risen; I am now experiencing an extremely confused sea, because the wind has changed from north to east. It is still blowing force 7 and, for this time of year, the weather is bitterly cold. The swells, with the wave and whitecap, have given way to huge rising and falling cones. Angry little spittles of white spray at the peaks disappear into the wind. All over the black surface of the water are silver veins of foam. Every now and then, just to let me know it's aware I'm intruding, the sea will send a full-blown wave crashing against Serenity, sending about twelve inches of green water cascading over the deck and cabin trunk. It's like turquoise stained glass as I look up through the skylight.

I love the sea, for reasons that I cannot explain. I am not frightened, although I certainly have had my moments of terror. No, my relationship with the sea is one of a worthy adversary in a basic game of survival. Over the long run, I know I can't win, but maybe I can settle for a draw. The contest sets the

*juices flowing and more than substitutes for the
intricate paper wars I left back in the boardrooms.*

*In the business world I must constantly succeed, I
must win more often than I lose. There is this ever-
present fear of failure; because of my inability or
unwillingness to shake the values of the world of
commerce, these attitudes and concerns carry over
into my personal life.*

*Once the land has disappeared over the horizon,
however, it is just me, my boat, and the sea. It is a
microcosm of life with the complexities removed.
For me this has had a purging effect. It has, because
of the necessity of staying alive, erased all extraneous
matters from my life and forced me to concentrate
on the exercise at hand. On Bay Street, in New York
or London, I am playing the game according to the
rules and the conventions established by society. Out
here, I go through a cleansing process which rids
both the mind and soul of things of questionable
value and brings into sharp focus those parts of my
life that are important and dear to me.*

*After clearing away the debris of my fifty-three
years of programmed thinking and values, I have
come to a very simple conclusion: success,
accolades, pride, material and sensual satisfaction are
worth striving for. But in more than thirty years in
the business community and family life, I have
gradually put these and other objectives ahead of the
two essential ingredients of my life from which all
forms of gratification are born: God and Love. I am
not proselytizing, and if those two words cause you
some embarrassment I am sorry, and I am sorry for
you. At this very moment, waiting for a rescue that
may never come, I am in a position to judge myself,
and myself alone. Under similar circumstances you
would possibly come to another conclusion but I can
assure you, you would come to a conclusion.*

*Although I have been aware of the existence of
God all my life, I now know that he is the very fibre,
essence, and reason for my being. For me it has been*

impossible to separate this world of the sea – His private world – from my presence in it.

Of equal and related importance is Love. I don't mean sexual love, although that forms a part of it. I mean the honest, deep, tender ability to care and be cared for. I have been unable to do this for many years. To be loved merely put me under an obligation that interfered with the progress of those important matters and preoccupations that have moulded me into what I am today.

One reason I left Bay Street and ventured into the Atlantic alone on a thirty-foot boat was because I was confused; the uncontaminated life on the sea was appealing. Without love and without God, life was beginning to hold and offer less and less, as the events and opportunities of the structured world unfolded. I wanted God, but I didn't have time for Him. I wanted to love and to be loved, but there were too many more important things going on. My life was filling to the brim with meaningless activities that provided neither food nor satisfaction for my inner being.

Through this complex and devious route, I have distilled my motives down to a deep and sincere hope that this experience will provide, through God, the ability, willingness, and power to love and be loved.

I do not know the answer. I do know, however, that when I return, if I return, I will have changed. . . .

Those were my thoughts at that moment.

CHAPTER TWELVE

*T*WO WEEKS OF DRIFTING HAD CREATED ITS OWN *ROUTINE. BECAUSE THERE WAS NO ELECTRICAL* power, lights, or radio, I rose and retired with the sun, spending much of my time between dusk and dawn reading. It was September 21, I still had lots of water – the port tank was full – and food for perhaps eight meals. I had been rationing myself one meal a day, six days a week, fasting on the seventh, a self-imposed asceticism that was no great hardship, given my indifference to food and my pronounced dislike of cooking it.

Of more concern than the impending end of my food supplies was the steady drop in temperature. The last two mornings there had been a thin skiff of ice on the trunk roof, and a dousing by a wave could be a painfully numbing experience. Even my warmest clothing was proving inadequate to keep out the damp wind when I was on deck, and the cold seemed to insinuate itself into every cranny of the cabin. The ocean was sucking heat out of the hull, and only bursts of heat from the stove beat back the chill. I spent much of my spare time (what an ironic term from someone stranded in a drifting boat!) on the bunk, wrapped in a blanket, re-reading my sailing books, dictating my journal, and reading the Bible. I had been through it once and had reached Paul's first letter to the Corinthians on my second pass.

I could feel the wind increasing, piling up the waves outside, trough to crest forty feet or more, and I knew I'd better get some hot food into me before cooking – or eating – became out of the question. But before I set the book aside, I twice read through the lilting and powerful poetry of Paul's message about love:

If I speak in the tongues of men and of angels,
but have not love, I am a noisy gong or a clanging

cymbal. And if I have prophetic powers, and understand all mysteries and all knowledge, and if I
have all faith, so as to remove mountains, but have
not love, I am nothing. If I give away all I have,
and if I give my body to be burned, but have not
love, I gain nothing.

If I had a chance to do it over, I would have done the obvious, practical things – inspected my sail before leaving, installed a diesel-powered generator, carried a single side bank
radio. But most important, I would have said good-bye – good-
bye to Wanda, Stephen, and Wendy, and hugged each of them
for a long, long time.

I was pensive and mellow as I prepared and ate my evening
meal of Danish cocktail sausages in warm skimmed milk and
granola; and I took a moment to give thanks for the spartan inventory of the Antiguan supermarket as I downed a dessert of
canned apricots. I waited for the coffee water to boil and found
myself daydreaming, summoning up memories: business lun-
cheons at Winston's, family skiing in Vermont, retrieving
Wendy from her ballet classes in the local church basement,
board meetings in our Grosvenor Street office, making love,
through-the-night negotiations, Christmases, my father's
smile, chilly afternoons watching Stephen's school soccer
team in action, quiet moments with Wanda. All gossamer
dramas with invisible players.

The wind came up howling out of the north that morning,
overtaking the beautiful, relatively calm weather of the
previous day. We had enjoyed a light breeze and brilliant sun
and I had rinsed out some underwear in a little fresh water (a
reckless gesture that did wonders for my morale) and dried it
on the main-sheet. In my journal it was almost possible to
forget that I was stranded and in very real danger of staying
that way permanently:

> The Lord has seen fit to give all of us here in the
> centre of the South Atlantic a most magnificent day.
> The sea is sparkling below the soft air; the sky is the
> kind of blue that you know there is more blue
> behind it.

157

But that next morning, the rounded, bruise-coloured cloud banks had started to plow the waves into mountains and by dusk my only wish was to make a mug of hot coffee before I retired. There was still more than an hour of light left, but the warmest place was in my bunk. I rinsed out my dish, racked it, and turned my attention to the kettle swinging on its gimballed burner: it seemed to be taking its sweet time boiling, I thought. I turned up the heat, but the flame just popped in puffy, yellow bursts.

It couldn't be! Not the propane. My other tank had lasted sixty days, in fact, it had run out only a week earlier. But then it dawned on me just how much gas I'd been using, relying on the stove for heat. That first tank served only for occasional cooking in the more tropical latitudes. During the past week's glacial winds, I'd been nipping below to warm myself, and the stove had been called into service more and more, to fend off the cold in the cabin and to cook hot meals. And now it was finished. No power, no radio, no engine, no sails – and now, no heat.

I hadn't been melodramatic when there was fuel, and I saw no reason to start now that I'd run out; but I wasn't fooling myself. I asked my silent crew, "How long do I have left? Three days? Four? Perhaps more, but not many more. . . ." I'm amazed now at how calm I felt. I may have mused about how tough I might be, and how long I could keep the cold from killing me; but I had left Halifax knowing that I was taking major risks, and now I was finding out what those risks would cost. Obviously, there was no point sitting in the middle of the ocean ringing my hands, unless it was to keep them warm a while longer. I was in a tranquil and resigned frame of mind when I retired to bed.

I didn't dictate a journal entry, although I'd been religious about that, and I made only a fitful stab at reading. The last short hour of light cast a bleary glow through the portholes, and I augmented it with the flashlight, which seemed to be the only mechanical thing on board that was still working, apart from the sextant.

I lay on my back with my head cradled in my arms and stared at the bulkhead. From the first day I'd been immobilized, I'd felt the abrupt end of the journey far more keenly than the possible end of my life. After the storms I'd weathered and the cleansing process I'd experienced, the tragedy was that it was over. Capetown, the Indian Ocean, the Roaring 40s, Melbourne, and the ultimate test, Cape Horn – all would remain legends unlived.

I was in the privileged position of knowing that I was going to die. I was not being dragged through the agony of a terminal illness, grief-stricken relatives, remorse, or even fear – all the usual preludes to the final moment. I wanted desperately to live, and I intended to do everything within my power to do so; but death had always been waiting as a fair and just alternative to the safe completion of the voyage. The trip had been the thing and I reluctantly accepted I might be called upon to pay the fare. The drama, which appears fraudulently melodramatic in retrospect, was lost on me. I knew there was no hope of rescue. I was headed for the floes of the Antarctic and oblivion.

Because *Serenity* was at the mercy of the waves, there was none of the muted, rhythmical music of water sliding along the hull as the bow cuts the waves. The cadence was quite different, but in its own way musical: a staccato slapping and breaking, as the boat and its fittings roared and whistled. *Serenity* and I had been through so many storms and knock-downs, and I had absolute confidence in her. As I huddled in the blankets, it was like the childhood comfort of being cuddled during a thunderstorm. The sounds dropped away one by one: first the slatting of the rigging, then the groan of the mast in its collar, then the very wind itself . . . .

An animal-like scream jerked me awake.

I couldn't tell where the sound had come from, although it was outside the cabin. I looked at my watch, vaguely aware that it was light. The time was just 1730 hours; I'd slept only twenty minutes or so, although it seemed like all night.

The sound was probably a seabird, I reasoned, an albatross or one of those damned boobies that carry on as though the weather is irrelevant to them. I hadn't seen a living thing in weeks and there was still enough light to go topside and take a look at a bird or, as a less exciting alternative, secure some lashing that may have broken loose.

The sun was a soft-focus ochre ball peeking briefly beneath

the stormy ceiling before dropping behind the horizon. With my arms propped loosely on the campanionway runners and my head just above the deck, I casually scanned the heaving grey world about me. I froze. There, standing off my starboard quarter and not half a mile away, glowing golden in the dying light, was a ship.

I clambered out into the cockpit and stood stunned as it was obscured by a wave mountain and then rose into view again. There was another blast from the siren (*that* was the scream) followed by a puff of black diesel smoke from her funnel as she revved her engines. I clipped on my safety harness, braced one leg against the wheel, and slowly raised my extended arms above my head and lowered them again, again, and again, in the universal signal of distress. If the master of that vessel saw it, he was obliged by international law to help me. Yet in those seas, I wouldn't have blamed him for cursing this lunatic sailor's amateur folly and pretending he didn't notice me in the waves. Pulling a man off a tiny boat in a gale is more than an inconvenience; it's a threat to both vessels.

Another small puff of black smoke rose from the funnel, followed by another and then a steady stream. She was underway – but leaving me. I raced below and re-emerged with my waterproof bag of flares and a Very pistol. The orange smoke from my daylight distress signal whipped downwind from my right hand, a brilliant red flame spluttered from the flare in my left. My rescue vessel was hull-down on the horizon, showing me her stern as my pyrotechnics expired.

CHAPTER THIRTEEN

SERENITY *AND I WERE ALONE ONCE AGAIN. THE VESSEL THAT HAD BEEN SO CLOSE WAS NOW MERGING WITH* the waves on the horizon; only her superstructure was silhouetted against the darkening sky. A desperate panic knotted my stomach as I saw my prospective rescuers steaming indifferently away.

But I knew that the captain had more than one way to pick me up – if he was going to pick me up. The easiest for him, but most dangerous for me, was "let the little guy take his chances." This option was to approach from downwind and let my boat float into his. The safer but more difficult way was for the rescue vessel to come down from the windward side, putting my much smaller boat in her lee, in effect providing a break-wall for me.

The *Masirah*, as I later found out, was skippered by Captain Polson, a superb seaman who intended to give me every break. She was now north of me and slightly to the west of the eye of the gale. I saw her turn. Slowly she bore down on me parallel to the line of the wind, heading for a point about half a mile off my starboard quarter. She slowed with the wind on her stern; staccato dots of grey erupted from her funnel as the wheelhouse called for reverse until she lay stationary in the water.

The sun was below the horizon and *Masirah* glowed motionless above the darkening water. Suddenly I was pinned by a huge search light. It was too early for the beam to be of any assistance, but it was apparent that they had no intention of letting me out of their sight as the night approached. The funnel puffed business-like balls of black smoke as her engines eased her forward. While seeming to remain in the same spot, she swung her bow ever so slowly to port until she was at right angles to me. It took *Masirah* almost an hour to manoeuvre herself into a position upwind from me and ready to move in for the rescue.

I learned later that Rob Brindle, the officer of the watch aboard M.V. *Masirah*, hadn't actually seen my little boat. What caught his attention, in the dusk, was a movement against the sky that was neither sea nor cloud. Ever since my sail had torn itself to shreds, half of it had flown in tattered streamers from the masthead, fifty-four feet above the deck. Although *Serenity*'s hull was virtually indistinguishable from the whitecaps, those streamers called for a second look. Peering through his binoculars, Brindle was able to identify *Serenity*'s hull as it rose into sight atop one of the great swells. It is ironic that the torn sail, the same sail that had caused my misadventure, was the instrument of my rescue. Without that great white flag on the horizon almost sixty feet above the sea, *Serenity*'s hull would have been just another white speck on the face of the vast Atlantic.

"I've sighted a small yacht, sir, maybe abandoned. No one seems to be aboard," Brindle said to Magnus Polson, the master of *Masirah*, who had come onto the bridge to check on the storm's fury.

"Ease in close, Mr. Brindle," said Captain Polson, taking up his binoculars and sweeping the area until he picked out my boat.

Approaching to within a half mile, *Masirah*'s siren gave out a near-bottomless, hollow "bow-ooooo--m." It wasn't a minute before Brindle saw the companionway door slide open. Then I appeared in my yellow storm suit.

"We've got a live one," said Brindle. "Let's try to raise him on the radio." *Masirah*'s radio operator, Paul Hartwell, called up to Brindle that he had already tried VHF 16 and MF 2182 and got no response; he ventured that my set was not operating.

"We'll come alongside him, Mr. Brindle," said Captain Polson. "We've got to get upwind. Put her on a course of 010."

As the *Masirah* swept past *Serenity* to start working back upwind, Brindle could see my Canadian ensign flown upside down and make out the yacht's name. "*Serenity . . . Serenity IV . . .* out of Toronto. She's a damned long way from home," he said to no one in particular.

I was a long way from home, in the middle of the South

Atlantic, 2,000 miles off the coast of Africa, a like distance from South America. I was quite probably the farthest from human habitation that anyone could be in this world. I had been found, through no effort of mine, by a ship. In this vast waste of sky and water, where not even seabirds seem to venture, we had met as if on a country road. The likelihood of such an encounter had to be a million to one. I stood transfixed, watching, as the drama played itself out.

Once *Masirah* had stationed herself between me and the gale she started to zigzag fore and aft, gradually moving her huge bulk downwind toward me. If my engine had been operating I could have powered right up alongside and saved her an hour or more of agonizing manoeuvring. The wind was actually drawing me farther away and the skipper had to take that into consideration. Tim Read, the chief engineer, handled his engines superbly in response to the captain's signals. The 10,500-ton freighter, moving relentlessly sideways, gradually gained on *Serenity* as we both slid downwind under the force of the gale. The sun was now long gone and, except for that illuminated stretch of water between the two vessels, the sky and the sea were of the same inky blackness. *Masirah*'s searchlight almost blinded me; although I could not see her hull, I could make out deck lights sparkling on the surface of the sea and above: she was gaining.

For weeks I'd been sailing the Southern Ocean on swells that I'd logged at anywhere between twenty and forty feet. For the first time I could relate these great rolling monsters to something of comparable scale, the *Masirah*. *Serenity* rose as *Masirah* fell – the vertical distance was easily sixty feet.

The gale, which had been blowing steadily at about force eight from the north, began to drop without warning. After a few moments of relative calm the wind moved in from the south. Polson had manoeuvered his vessel so that the wind passed over and around the larger ship, creating a vacuum that would suck *Serenity* into the *Masirah*'s lee. We began to close rapidly.

I was now a hundred yards away and could see the great hull and the movement on her decks; I caught the sound of her engines throbbing above the roar of the sea.

Fifty yards: diesel fumes and excited voices blew across the light-specked water. The throbbing, clanking, and rattling of a ship at work engulfed us.

I could see that a line had been strung from bow to stern, draped to the waterline (although in those huge swells the waterline was a purely arbitrary benchmark). I could see figures crowded along the rails. Were they passengers? Did they speak English? Where would I sleep? These and other trivia raced through my mind when I should have been giving my total attention to a life-and-death struggle.

Finally, I was close enough to take a ridiculously simple Lake Ontario boat hook, snag the yellow bow-to-stern line, and loop a rope of my own over it. I left plenty of spare line coiled on the deck in anticipation of what was going to happen. As the swells rolled by, the two vessels rose and fell asynchronously. *Serenity* shot up the side of *Masirah* at breakneck speed, then hurtled down again as *Masirah* rose. One moment, I was staring into the eyes of an East Indian deckhand; the next, I was looking up at *Masirah*'s black underside. There were horrible, heart-rending grinding and tearing sounds as the rivets and steel hull of the larger boat bit deeply into *Serenity*'s delicate teak and fibreglass. A couple of ladders dropped over the side and I saw men with hands cupped to their mouths, but their shouts were snatched away by the reappearance of the force eight wind, the sounds of the engines, and the grating of the two hulls tearing at each other.

Suddenly, at one of my high-level pauses, the chief mate, Andy Pritchard, vaulted from his deck and landed, cat-like, on mine. He had no life jacket and no safety line; dressed in green oilskins, he acted as if he was out on a quiet country walk on a rainy Sunday. Extending his hand, Pritchard said casually, "Well now, what can we do for you?"

"By God, I'm glad to see you." I rushed on, "I've got some gear onboard, already packed. I know you're not obliged to take anything but me. . . ."

"No problem," smiled Pritchard, and jerked his hand towards *Masirah*'s deck. Instantly, the East Indian crewmen who lined the ship's rail rained down a dozen catlines on us; several of them whacked me pretty hard.

As the vessels rocketed vertically past each other, tethered only by a straining line, I ducked below and heaved my bags out into the cockpit.

164

Weeks earlier, I had divided my belongings into "essential," "almost essential," and "nice to have along." I packed them into three separate bags with a small suitcase left over for last-minute articles. Never having been rescued at sea before, I was trying to go about this logically. I had entertained vain hopes that *Serenity* might come along, too, if the rescue vessel could hoist her on deck. This was clearly impractical in this weather; besides, *Masirah* was too small. But my practical preparations made my personal rescue as uncomplicated as such a complicated venture can be.

I had had my "abandon ship instructions" taped just above the galley:

If a vessel responds:
1) Get dressed;
2) Collect extra items not packed;
3) Close luggage;
4) Close sea cocks: galley, vanity, head (2);
5) Take down ensign;
6) Padlocks;
7) Ventilator caps;
8) Take 3 articles of luggage:
    1 chart case
    1 tote bag
    1 suit bag

This may appear as if I had merely distracted myself while having nothing better to do than make lists. At this moment, however, exhilarated at the prospect of rescue, bleary with exhaustion, preoccupied with the minutiae of making and retaining contact, it proved a prudent bit of planning. I ducked below from time to time as *Masirah* edged towards me, and by the time Pritchard landed beside me, everything was packed neatly, ready to go.

Items one, two, and three are obvious. The closing of the sea cocks can prevent flooding. The padlocks had nothing to do with vandalism (it would take a hardy vandal to brave the South Atlantic), but assured that all exterior hinged openings would remain shut in any storms the abandoned boat might experience. The ventilator hoods were removed and water-tight caps put in place for the same reason. I was giving *Seren-*

ity a fighting chance at survival, although I couldn't imagine what form such survival would take.

The ensign was quite a bit worse for wear, but it had been through a lot with me and held more than a little sentimental value.

Pritchard seemed most concerned about my safety, although I was the one with the life jacket and safety harness, and he insisted that I get off while he saw to the removal of my gear.

I knotted one of the lines from the freighter around my waist and detached my harness for the last time. I timed my departure as *Serenity* rose on a swell. It was imperative that I make my move at the crest of the cycle, that I grasp the rope ladder just as the boat started down, dropping from beneath my feet. A miscalculation could result in *Serenity* crushing me against the steel hull on her upward surge to the top.

There was a slight weightlessness underfoot as she started her downward plunge. I leaned out for the rungs of the ladder. Four or five quick steps and I was pulled to safety by a hundred friendly hands.

A few days later I read a portion of *Masirah's* log:

> *1723 hours yacht sited by Rob Brindle, officer of watch, stand by main engine. 1733 stop main engine. 1735 to 1913 manoeuvering alongside yacht. 1913 heaving line onboard yacht. 1921 David Philpott boarded the ship. 1925 'Serenity' set adrift and abandoned. Resumed passage to Durban. . . .*
>
> *On siting 'Serenity' course was altered to close by the Master, I [the chief mate] was called to the bridge. The Master decided to approach the starboard side to. I called the crew and cadets and rigged the pilot ladder and Jacob's ladder plus a boat rope. With a heaving line onboard the yacht, it was brought alongside and secured. No other gear was required but life jackets, rocket line, safety harness, and plenty of cat lines were on hand.*

I could have been rescued by anything that sailed the seven seas, but here I found myself surrounded by English-speaking officers aboard a trim and well-kept British merchant freighter. I kept hugging people out of sheer gratitude. They clustered around me, laughing and reaching out to shake my hand; and even in my dazed state, I began to understand that none of them had ever before been called to a sea rescue. It was almost as big a thrill for them to have rescued me as it was for me to have been rescued.

I continued to pump the hands of the white-uniformed officers until I noticed a cadre of beaming, swarthy sailors maintaining a respectful distance, but part of the whole joyous scene. I singled out a short, wiry East Indian whose muscle-knotted chest was just barely covered by an orange sleeveless shirt announcing that "Sailors do it better." I grabbed his hand in both of mine and looked down into his face. His eyes sparkled back at me, and the sinews in his neck were taut as he held a brilliant, uncontrollable smile. "I threw one of the lines, sir," he blurted out with obvious pride.

"Thank you!" I replied, with a lump in my throat.

Looking south, I watched *Serenity* in the glow of *Masirah*'s lights. She rose to the top of one of the great black swells – steady, mast vertical, bow pointed toward me. Then she dropped into the valley beyond. *Serenity* was gone, and I could not dwell on her loss.

CHAPTER FOURTEEN

*I*T WAS PAST MIDNIGHT WHEN THEY FINALLY LET ME
LEAVE THE WARDROOM AFTER TELLING AND RETELLING
the whole story of my journey and my disablement. First officer, second officers, third engineers, cadets – virtually the entire off-duty roster of *Masirah* crowded around me. "Did you think you would die?" "What was it like to be knocked down?" "How did you get the head wound?" "How much was the boat worth?" "Is Toronto on the sea?" "How many children do you have?" "What are you going to do now?" I lubricated the answers with hot soup.

When I was finally blind and giddy with fatigue, I was escorted to what was called the "owner's suite." There I found to my amazement that my cases had been unpacked, my pyjamas pressed and laid out, and a bath had been drawn – a huge bath, the biggest damn bath I'd ever seen – the fresh warm water sloshing around gently in defiant response to the violence of the seas outside. I sank into the tub with a groan of satisfaction.

A few hours earlier I had doubted that I'd survive, and now I found myself on a British merchant vessel with all the luxurious comforts of my euphoric dream.

My relief reflected the intense disquiet I'd obviously been keeping in pretty close check on board *Serenity*. I cried. Slipping from the bath and into my pressed pyjamas and that huge soft bed, I slept until ten a.m. the next morning.

As if divining that I was awake, the tiny East Indian steward appeared as I opened my eyes, bearing a large mug of milky coffee and a silver rack of dry toast. My clothes had been laid out on the couch, and it was all I could do to believe I was really there. As I sat in bed, munching my toast and sipping the coffee, I discovered Canadian motifs all around me. There were maple leaf inlays in the floors, and pictures of Indians, and Hudson's Bay traders marched in murals round the walls.

Of all the cockroach-ridden steamers on the seas, with all the pirates and reeking fishing boats and sterile supertankers, with all the "what ifs" of all the ships that might have picked me up, David Philpott's kismet had come through again. I have always had a feeling of destiny, of the rightness of things unfolding; and this wonderful ship with the Canadian decor seemed to confirm it.

I threw aside the covers and staggered from bed – the great ship's motion was far different from that of my tiny boat. I wasn't slept out; all through the night I had surfaced every two hours or so, as had become my habit, keeping an eye and an ear out for trouble. When I stretched and stood naked in front of a full-length mirror, I realized I was gaunt, down to one hundred and fifty pounds. I hadn't looked much worse after my punishing Florida bike trek.

I resolved to pack away some heavy-duty calories and set off for the wardroom, where I was served a gargantuan breakfast. As it was nearly eleven a.m., the kitchen crew was already preparing the midday food; but they hovered over me with all the solicitude of doting grandmothers. Hotcakes, sausages, eggs, and what seemed like gallons of coffee were spread in front of me with baked goods of every description.

My diet during the last two weeks on *Serenity* had been deficient in some areas, notably greens and carbohydrates. I craved bread, butter, pastries, fresh fruit, and salad. I ate the equivalent of two or three full meals at each of three daily sittings aboard *Masirah*, much to the amusement and encouragement of the officers and galley staff. (I have a suspicion they ran pools on just how much I would eat!)

After breakfast, I was invited to the captain's cabin for a chat, for he and I had spoken only briefly when I was welcomed aboard. He showed me the cables he had sent on his own behalf and at my request the night before. The one to Lloyd's of London, the insurer, read:

RESCUED ONE YACHTSMAN DAVID PHILPOTT CANADIAN
CITIZEN FROM YACHT SERENITY IV OF TORONTO STOP YACHT
NOW ABANDONED IN POSITION 32° 23 MINUTES SOUTH 18° 17

MINUTES WEST STOP YACHT HAS BEEN DISABLED SEVENTEEN
DAYS STOP NOW PROCEEDING DURBAN ETA 282100 – MASTER.

Captain Polson had also alerted Capetown radio:

THIRTY FOOT FIBERGLASS YACHT SERENITY IV OF TORONTO
ABANDONED IN POSITION 32° 23 MINUTES SOUTH 18° 17
MINUTES WEST AND NOW DRIFTING AFTER PICKING UP ONE
SURVIVOR STOP HULL AND CABIN WHITE AND BOTTOM BLUE
STOP – MASTER.

He also showed me the cable he sent to Wanda and one to
his headquarters, the Cunard Lines in Bristol, signalling that
he'd been detained more than two hours to pick me up. I asked
how much he thought that might have cost him; he reckoned
it at about £2,000 in fuel and lost time, adding hastily that it
was just one of the many imponderables of maritime business.

He willingly sent another cable to Lloyd's giving details of
my passport, the yacht registry, dates of sailing and disablement, and another cable via Capetown to Toronto letting my
office know I was safe and well. This last message got somewhat garbled somewhere along its transmission, and by the
time Joan Hammell got it, I was safely aboard a Portuguese
fishing boat!

After the cables had been dispatched, I related my story to
Captain Polson. He was a quiet, contemplative man, who
tended to let the story unfold in its own way, interjecting only
a terse question now and again to keep the facts straight. He
seemed only mildly interested in my history before *Serenity*,
especially my business, which seemed peculiar because on
Bay Street you are what you do. Polson was far more concerned to learn the tiny details of my sailing, without being
critical or condescending.

"Well, you'll want to be looking around the ship," he said,
slapping his chair arms to signal the end of our chat. "You
have the run of it. Ask Mr. Brindle to look to your needs, or
Mr. Pritchard. You'll join our table for meals, of course. We
should be putting into Durban in about a week."

As I stepped from the master's cabin, I could feel the breeze
in my face; and I couldn't help noting ruefully that this very
wind should have been moving me towards Capetown at a re-

170

spectable seven and a half knots, if everything had worked out according to plan.

I found *Masirah* a relatively informal ship. Within a day I was on first-name terms with all the officers except the captain. I learned from Ken Gaskell, the purser, that *Masirah* had been launched by the Cunard Lines as the *Port Alfred* in 1960, to make the Richelieu, Quebec, to London run; later she carried frozen meat and dairy products from Australia and New Zealand to Britain. Its original mandate explained the ship's decor of Indians, maple leaves, and other Canadiana, although they became an anachronism after the ship was re-christened *Masirah* in 1978. It was now under charter to a Brazilian company, en route to Iraq with a cargo of chickens.

The crew, deck, and engine-room gangs, stewards, kitchen help, and other hands were mostly East Indians or from the Persian Gulf. The officers and cadets were all British career merchant-navy men. I don't have a lot of experience with these things, but it seemed to be a happy ship.

Masirah had a beam of sixty-seven feet, and every inch of it, except for necessary crew and engineering quarters, was chock full of frozen chickens: 411,584 cartons of them, ten to fourteen to a carton – more than five million birds. Of course I had to see this poultry spectacular as part of the bow-to-stern, deck-to-keel tour Andy Pritchard gave me, introducing me to the crew as we went.

Pritchard was unerringly kind and friendly, going far beyond what would have been expected of him in looking after a castaway. For instance, I had asked him to confirm an inventory of the gear I'd brought aboard, for the insurance claim I'd be making. The next day I found a neatly typed inventory signed by Pritchard and Captain Polson waiting in my stateroom.

When we came across Rob Brindle, Pritchard told me that, in addition to his reputation for being a superior second officer, Brindle was famous on Cunard ships for inventing the nautical banana, a high-tech unit of measurement by which the crew managed to pass the time guesstimating how many standard banana cartons it would take to stretch end-to-end from Auckland to Southampton or how many would stack to the moon.

My tour with Pritchard confirmed my view that a ship is

one of the two most beautiful man-made objects, the other being the airplane. The aesthetic appeal is indistinguishable from function, from the rhythmic throbbing of the giant diesels to the no-nonsense lines of the hull.

As we clambered up and down ladders and in and out of hatches, Pritchard told me that he'd been in the shower when Rob Brindle spotted *Serenity*; he'd just thrown on his clothes and dashed up to the bridge. Although Captain Polson handled the manoeuvring of the vessel, it was Pritchard's duty as chief officer to direct the rescue. He admitted, rather sheepishly, that in the excitement he had broken one of the most basic rules by leaping onto my boat without a safety line or life jacket. "It was my first time," he laughed. That may be, but he and his fellow officers had been subjected to the kind of rigorous training that makes such heroics second nature.

Pritchard said that when trainees enter the merchant service, usually between sixteen and nineteen years of age, they elect whether to become deck officers, as he had, or engineering officers. The former allows them to secure a master's certificate and take full control of a vessel. The latter course can lead to a chief's certificate, making you king of the underworld, so to speak: the engine room, refrigeration, electrical system, and so on. The advantage to becoming an engineer is that a few years at sea gives one training that can also be profitable on land, while a deck officer is limited to maritime-related work. However, judging from what I'd seen, if a deck officer from Cunard applied to me for a job, I'd have no trouble accepting his qualifications for an executive position.

I felt a certain envy when Pritchard and some of the other men rambled on about their careers, adventures, and lifestyles. These were real men – mariners, seamen, and voyagers – heroes of which legends are made.

Paradoxically, it was I who received the hero's treatment. *Masirah* had originally been equipped as a passenger/cargo ship, and the stewards treated me as an honoured guest. My laundry was done, my suit was pressed, my land shoes sparkled. Morning and evening there was a hot bath, and tea was delivered bedside as I towelled off.

One of the great characters I met was the chief, Tim Read, a big, bluff, good-natured sort who ranked equally with the master but ruled below-decks with his staff of five engineers. It was Tim who had pinned me with that blinding searchlight as the rescue progressed. "I don't mind saying I cursed you out because it didn't look as though you were doing anything for yourself," he said in mock seriousness. As I began to bluster an explanation, he laughed and told me it didn't take long to realize I was without power. "We saw you trying to wave the light away, but Pritchard said 'Keep it on him.' We didn't want to lose your company."

It was Tim who told me that Andy Pritchard very nearly didn't make it back aboard on the night of the rescue. *Serenity* suddenly swerved away from *Masirah*, and Pritchard had to leap across a yawning gap of open water to grab the ladder. Had *Serenity* rushed back, she might have crushed him. As it was, when the hull of my little boat swerved away, her mast raked *Masirah*'s teak rail. If Read hadn't foreseen the possibility of a serious accident and ordered everyone back, the swinging spar would have clipped the heads off one and all standing there taking in the show.

I had taken Captain Polson at his word and roamed at will about the ship. I was drawn back time and again to the bridge. The gyro compass was being serviced (*Masirah* was showing her age: the compass was run by a motor cannibalized from a floor polisher!) and the ship's wheel was on manual. It was a unique thrill handling a 10,500-ton vessel in a high sea with a force six wind off the beam and a Cunard officer at my shoulder.

The *Masirah*'s bridge was forty-six feet above the water and gave me a visible radius of more than eight miles. On *Serenity*, on a clear day, my eyeline was seven feet above the surface, giving a horizon about three miles away. The sight from the bridge of this vast, raging sea of incalculable power gave me an awesome new perspective on my voyage. Yet when I descended to the lower deck, the swells once again obstructed my vision, the raging plane of whitecaps was again obscured, and the sensation of uncontrolled violence disappeared. This is undoubtedly how I had been able to accept the sea as a worthy but not unfriendly adversary from *Serenity*'s cockpit: I had no idea what fury surrounded me. Had I been able to hover over the masthead during any of the storms, I can imagine that the heart might have gone from me in terror. During the eighty-one days that I was at sea, from the time I left Halifax, I experienced seventeen gales of force seven or higher. What I saw from the bridge was what I was unable to see at the time. Thank God!

One of the unexpected pleasures of being aboard *Masirah* was the easy way these career navy men accepted me as one of their own. The day Andy Pritchard said, "Well, of course, from one seaman to another . . ." I felt my ego do a half turn and give me a big smile. The distance I had sailed single-handed was my initiation. I asked Captain Polson what he honestly thought of yachtsmen venturing into waters normally the domain of vessels like his own.

"I think you're all mad," he said, with a slight smile flickering across his normally impassive face. "Most of us would never attempt it. The stamina and the skills are beyond us. Anyway, I'm not sure I'd like being on my own that long."

Andy Pritchard said he'd have been "bloody scared" to take on the Atlantic single-handed.

I had an inexplicable sense of fulfilment being accepted as a "seaman." It allowed me to share their fabled world for a time. When I went on the bridge, Rob Brindle took me to the chart table and assumed I understood what was going on. I was even allowed to take over watches on the bridge. Granted, I had an officer to call on, but I found I could handle a vessel of this size, direct the helmsman, do the plotting, and operate from the radar through a whole night's watch. Daytime watches were a piece of cake – all visual. I had already found and demonstrated that those hundreds of sextant sights on *Serenity* had honed my navigation skills almost to the equal of these college-trained officers.

It was customary for the officers and cadets of *Masirah* to dine together in the smallish dining room each night, with Captain Polson presiding. Afterwards we would adjourn to the lounge for drinks, talk, and sometimes a film (the second night aboard I saw *Dirty Harry* with Clint Eastwood).

One evening I took Tim Read aside after dinner to ask a question that had been nagging at me.

"You know these waters. What are the chances of my boat being picked up?"

"I wouldn't expect any miracles – don't get your hopes up. She'll soon be moving into the Roaring 40s. With her skipper at the helm, well, she might have had a chance. Alone, she'll probably break up or bury herself in the Antarctic ice."

I didn't really expect anything else, but the stark hearing of it left me disquieted and sad.

Another thing I learned in the lounge that night was that Iraq and Iran had gone to war, and this was complicating *Masirah*'s voyage no end. The frozen chickens were to be delivered to Basrah, Iraq, some seventy-five miles up the Shatt al Arab River, which formed part of the embattled border. That all crew would receive double pay while in an area of hostilities didn't dispel their feelings of concern and tension.

I was luxuriating in my big, beautiful bath on the evening of September 25 when the radio operator, Paul Hartwell, came rushing into the cabin with word that a reporter was on the wireless from South Africa wanting to speak to me. My suggestion that he call back didn't have any effect so, dripping wet and wrapped in a towel, I answered such disjointed and baffling questions as "Did I own the *Masirah*?" and "Was I alive on my own boat when I was rescued?" I tried to straighten him out, but I imagine his readers were as baffled as I.

The next day, more calls. First some quack out of Capetown, who said he was from Pennsylvania and wanted to salvage *Serenity*. I agreed to meet him through the Lloyd's agent in Durban when I arrived; but nothing came of it. Then the South African correspondent for an Indian newspaper called; our conversation was, if possible, even more garbled and hilariously misunderstood than the first interview.

I was on the bridge exactly five days to the hour after I'd been sighted when I saw the first blip on the radar screen that indicated the coast around Capetown. The officer of the watch told me we'd see land later that evening. I asked him how one distinguished the real from the imaginary in the flurry of snow on the radar screen. He said it was extremely difficult, if not impossible, to spot a vessel as small as *Serenity*, which carried a proper radar reflector. On the screen, even a floating albatross can read like a small boat, and there is a tendency not to check out these blips in open water because the likelihood of coming across a small vessel far from land is slight. A ship could waste all its time running around the ocean chasing ghosts born of the limitations and deficiencies of radar. How lucky I was that it had been daylight with Rob Brindle alert on the bridge! The capriciousness of radar gave me great sympathy for the skipper of a large vessel manoeuvring in crowded waters.

At 2145 hours on September 25 I had the thrill of seeing my first sign of land since leaving Antigua. I caught a flashing light off the port beam, and ran up to the bridge to catch the whole story on the chart and radar. Soon we were moving through waters where buoys, shore lights, and other vessels were all around us, and it was fascinating to compare the observations from the bridge wings with the radar, and the plotting charts and with the Decca read-outs.

In the water all around *Masirah* glowed a broad wreath of greenish, white phosphoresence. On *Serenity* I'd seen this phenomenon only fleetingly as little blobs of light quickly extinguished in the wake.

I spent the first part of the evening on the bridge with Mark Gooderham, a cadet who was looking forward to his leave. He was heading straight home to Lilongwe, Malawi, the Central African nation that had been Nyasaland in my high school geography lessons.

After Mark's shift, Will Headon took over and continued my education in the mysteries of the Decca electronic navigation. Will was third officer and had brought his wife Rosemary along. She shared part of each watch with him and provided us with bacon-and-egg sandwiches at four in the morning. The Headons kept me company often during the trip, and their *Field Guide to Seabirds* answered questions about the birds that had performed spectacular aerobatics around *Serenity*.

The largest bird was a Wandering Albatross, with an eleven-foot wingspan and a range all over the southern hemisphere, south of the Tropic of Capricorn. The beautiful white, long-tailed bird that flew above my mast between Bermuda and Antigua was a Tropic Bird. And the beasts that took possession of the boat in the Doldrums at the beginning of August were, indeed, Brown Boobies. Mine had probably never seen a human being before and chose this as reason to celebrate.

Will and Rosemary talked to me about their life and their home in Horndean, Portsmouth. I found myself able to open up to these people in a way I'd never been able to do before, to talk and to establish a relationship with virtual strangers in an easy, informal manner. All my executive life I had trained myself to posture defensively, to avoid personal involvements, and to keep up my guard. Yet these people accepted me, the stranger plucked from the sea, without giving a damn whether I was president of this or chairman of that. We talked instead about real things, about feelings and aspirations, about God, society, and politics, about the beautiful and the tragic. They, and the others, had unknowingly been my bridge from solitude to my new world.

Tim Read, the chief, who had led me through the labyrinth of pipes, machinery, and pistons that made up *Masirah*'s power plant; Andy Pritchard, who made me feel like a real seaman; Robert Brindle, the officer that first saw *Serenity*; Ken Gaskell, the amiable purser; Paul Hartwell, whose wireless re-established my contact with the world; Polson, Nichols, Hoyle and his wife Andrea, Sibbering, Ibbotson, Garner, Tomlinson, Barlow, and the rest aboard the *Masirah*.

That I had been denied my goal of shepherding *Serenity* into the calm of Capetown harbour no longer seemed significant. The real achievement had been the successful sailing, navigating and surviving more than 7,300 nautical miles of river and ocean, 6,000 single-handed. There would be no prize, no bottom line profit; nor did I expect anything more than the most cursory recognition from my peers. But I was contented, fulfilled. The experience of the voyage and the privilege of being accepted as a seafaring man by career mariners was more than enough compensation and plaudit.

There was a wonderful world out there to be embraced. With Cape Agulhas on the northern horizon, and the Atlantic astern, I looked ahead to the mist-shrouded surface of the Indian Ocean. I had left a voyage unfinished: there just might be another *Serenity*.

EPILOGUE

O N FEBRUARY 20, 1981, FIVE MONTHS TO THE DAY AFTER SERENITY *DISAPPEARED INTO THE RAGING* blackness of the South Atlantic, I received a telephone call from the Canadian Registrar of Shipping. A Brazilian freighter, the *Jurupeme*, was on her way to Japan with *Serenity IV* lashed safely on her deck.

Following my rescue, it was assumed that, in the unlikely case that *Serenity* remained afloat, she would continue south ahead of the gale; then, caught in the Falkland current and the West Wind Drift, she would be carried east past the tip of Africa to Australia or the Antarctic ice.

It appeared, however, that *Serenity* latched on to the cold Benguela current, on which she was bordering the night she was abandoned. The northerly gales probably carried her 500 to 800 miles farther south, the beginning of an 8,000-10,000 mile voyage in which *Serenity* swung in a 3,000-mile wide circle in the middle of the South Atlantic, propelled by winds and currents. If she did, in fact, follow this route at her earlier drifting speed of fifty-five miles per day, then it was quite reasonable that she would be sighted by the *Jurupema* within 700 miles of where she had been abandoned five months earlier. The real wonder was that she had survived the savage battering she must have absorbed in the Roaring 40s without sail or master. Photographs of *Serenity IV* on *Jurupema*'s deck showed her to be in good condition with only cosmetic damage to her hull; that was confirmed by later reports from the Japanese insurance inspector.

Just before her ghostly reappearance, I had completed my paperwork with Lloyd's of London and was about to receive my cheque for the loss of *Serenity*. But with the sudden appearance of invoices covering dry storage in Osaka, Japan, at

178

$1,000 per day, the insurers disappeared into their bureau-cratic cocoon. I might still be waiting for my money if I had not heard, quite fortuitously, that a Mr. Ollie Constable had taken possession of the boat in Osaka, transported it to his yard in Parry Sound, Ontario, made the necessary repairs, and sold her to a Mr. Ted Ayers of Indianola, Washington. I attached the boat with a court order, and within days I was fully compensated by Lloyd's.

It seems the thirty-footer has started a new life in Puget Sound, sailing as *Pole Cat*.

The name "Serenity IV" is mine for voyages yet to come.

Printed in Canada